YORK NOTES

General Editors: Professor A. N. Jeffares (University

The Belvedere Academy

This book is due for return on or before that last date shown below.

S

YORK PRESS
Immeuble Esseily, Place Riad Solh, Beirut.

LONGMAN GROUP LIMITED
Longman House, Burnt Mill, Harlow,
Essex CM20 2JE, England
and Associated Companies throughout the World.

© Librairie du Liban 1980

First published 1980
Reprinted 1984 and 1985
ISBN 0 582 78164 7
Printed in Hong Kong by
Sheck Wah Tong Printing Press Ltd

Contents

Part 1

Introduction

The life of Dickens

Charles Dickens was born at Portsmouth in 1812 and was the second child of John Dickens, a clerk in the Naval Pay Office. The family later moved to Chatham, where Charles started school, and finally to Camden Town, a poor suburb of London. In 1824 John Dickens got into serious financial trouble and was imprisoned for debt in the Marshalsea. Charles had to leave school and go to work in a blacking factory where he labelled bottles for wages of six shillings a week. After three months John Dickens was released from prison and Charles was sent to Wellington House Academy, a private school. Nevertheless, this brief period left a deep scar on Dickens's character. He was ashamed of having a father who had been to prison and he was humiliated by the hard manual work in the blacking factory. He was particularly hurt by his mother's apparent indifference to his sufferings.

In 1827, at the age of fifteen, Dickens went to work in a law firm. After learning shorthand, he turned to journalism, first as a freelance reporter and later as an employee of the *Morning Chronicle*. He specialised in reports of court cases and parliamentary debates. In 1829 he fell in love with Maria Beadnell, the daughter of a banker. The relationship continued until 1833 when it became clear that the Beadnells would not agree to the marriage. Meanwhile Dickens had begun to contribute humorous pieces to various periodicals: in 1836 they appeared in book form as *Sketches by Boz*. In the same year he married Catherine Hogarth, daughter of the editor of the *Evening Chronicle*.

Dickens was now commissioned to write another series of sketches which developed into his first novel, *The Pickwick Papers*. Like all Dickens's novels this was published first in instalments and later as a book (1837). *The Pickwick Papers* was a great success and established its author as a highly popular novelist. Two other events made 1837 an important year for Dickens. He established a close relationship with John Forster who became a trusted adviser and later wrote the first biography of Dickens. In May he was deeply moved by the death of his sister-in-law, Mary Hogarth, of whom he said 'I solemnly believe so perfect a creature never breathed'.

Between 1837 and 1841 Dickens wrote four successful novels: *Oliver Twist, Nicholas Nickleby, The Old Curiosity Shop,* and *Barnaby Rudge*. These novels added sentiment and melodrama to the humour of *The Pickwick Papers*. After a disappointing visit to America in 1842, Dickens returned to England to write *Martin Chuzzlewit* which proved less popular than his earlier work. In 1844, however, he reached a vast audience with his famous story, *A Christmas Carol*. Between 1844 and 1847 Dickens and his family travelled in Italy, Switzerland, and France.

The novels of Dickens's middle period are more serious in theme and more carefully constructed than his early work. After *Dombey and Son* (1846–8), Dickens turned to his own childhood and youth for the plot of *David Copperfield* (1849–50). The novels written between 1852 and 1857 (*Bleak House, Hard Times, Little Dorrit*) show the novelist's growing concern with social injustice and administrative inefficiency. Dickens had not lost his gifts as a public entertainer, but he now combined them with a genuine moral fervour.

At this time Dickens was personally involved in a number of philanthropic ventures. He took an active part in helping Miss Burdett Coutts to run a reform home for prostitutes and also supported the Administrative Reform Association. In 1848 Dickens began to organise and act in amateur theatrical performances for charitable purposes. In 1853 he gave his first public readings from his own works. These public readings were to prove popular and profitable, but they involved a physical strain which eventually undermined Dickens's health. To add to this already excessive activity, he founded in 1850 a weekly journal called *Household Words*. The contributors included not only Dickens himself, but also such distinguished literary figures as Mrs Gaskell, Bulwer Lytton, Charles Reade, and Wilkie Collins. In 1859 *Household Words* was succeeded by *All the Year Round* which achieved a circulation of three hundred thousand.

Catherine Hogarth had not proved an ideal wife for Dickens. She had given him ten children, but her placid nature had never adapted to the novelist's sensitive and exuberant character. In 1859 they separated. Dickens formed a new relationship with Ellen Ternan, a young actress who became his mistress but did not bring him real happiness. Dickens's last three novels were *A Tale of Two Cities* (1859), *Great Expectations* (1860–61), and *Our Mutual Friend* (1864–5). There is no sign of a declining talent: on the contrary, *Great Expectations* is often considered to be Dickens's finest novel. He had thus completed fourteen full-length novels in less than thirty years. To this intense creative work we must add his activity as journalist, actor, public reader and philanthropist. In 1867, despite increasing ill-health, Dickens travelled to America and gave public readings of his work. In 1870, after more readings in England, he began to write *The Mystery of Edwin Drood* which was never completed. In June 1870 he collapsed and died at his home in Kent. His death was an occasion for national mourning, and he was buried among the great writers of the past in Westminster Abbey.

The life and the novels

Even from such a brief biographical sketch, it should be clear that the novels of Dickens frequently reflect aspects of his own personal experience. This is obviously the case with *David Copperfield*, which, as a fictionalised autobiography, can be compared with such works as D.H. Lawrence's *Sons and Lovers* (1913) or James Joyce's *A Portrait of the Artist as a Young Man* (1916). Like the young Dickens, David absorbs imaginative literature, especially the early English novelists: like Dickens again, he suffers agonies of shame when he is sent to work in a factory: finally, he ends up by making his living as a writer. Dickens's father provides a partial model for the comically improvident Mr Micawber, and Maria Beadnell is recreated as David's child-wife, Dora. The other novels do not reflect Dickens's private life in such an obvious way. Nevertheless, the underlying themes still derive from crucial aspects of his own experience. As J. Hillis Miller has said, 'they are transformed into a "fable", perhaps, but they still retain the essential form of Dickens's sense of the meaning of his own life'.*

The fable essentially is the story of a lost or rejected child who endures intense suffering, both mental and physical, without losing his integrity; finally he discovers the secret of his identity and is rewarded with happiness and prosperity. One notices how close this scheme comes to the fairy-tale pattern of the humble hero or heroine who turns out to be a prince or a princess. *Oliver Twist, David Copperfield*, and *Bleak House* are all variations on this basic theme. *Great Expectations*, as we shall see, provides an unexpected critical perspective on the same fairy-tale plot. There can be no doubt that, in choosing stories of this kind, Dickens gives us his 'sense of the meaning of his own life'. It might be said, of course, that Dickens has an exaggerated reaction to the misfortunes of his own childhood. After all, his stay in the blacking factory lasted only a few months, and the vast majority of nineteenth-century English children lived in conditions that were a good deal worse.

*J. Hillis Miller, *Charles Dickens: the world of his novels*, Harvard University Press, Cambridge, Massachusetts, 1958, p.251.

But such considerations are hardly relevant. It was not the objective physical hardship of the factory that left a permanent mark on the novelist's mature imagination. What matters much more is what the factory episode meant for the young Dickens in terms of his view of society and his relationship with his parents. It showed him the vulnerability of innocence and the inability or unwillingness of society to protect a child from the consequences of his parents' mistakes. That is why so many children in the novels begin their lives as orphans or outcasts from society. The hero of *Oliver Twist*, Pip in *Great Expectations*, and Esther Summerson in *Bleak House* are all made to feel that society has no duties towards them. They are told from the start that they are an unwelcome burden for those who look after them: their very existence is presented to them as a source of guilt. In short, the major novels of Dickens reveal deep-rooted fears of isolation and insecurity caused originally by his insensitive mother and his improvident father. The episode of the blacking factory served Dickens as a kind of focus, a traumatic moment of awareness which hardened his childhood anxieties into a permanent frame of mind.

One obvious consequence of Dickens's attitude towards his own childhood is that he rarely presents satisfactory relations between parents and children. Instead, he prefers to concentrate on orphans such as Pip, Estella, and Magwitch in *Great Expectations*. On one level, this allows him to dramatise his own sense of isolation and insecurity. On another level, it suggests that he takes revenge on his own parents by excluding them from his fiction. By projecting himself into the obviously pathetic figure of the orphan, Dickens gains from his readers the sympathy he failed to receive during his childhood.

Dickens's novels also reflect certain aspects of his adult experience. Most critics have noticed that he seems almost incapable of dealing with sexual relationships. It is true, of course, that Victorian novelists were extremely reticent about sexual matters, but in Dickens the problem is not merely one of propriety or prudery. We need only think of his frustrated courtship of Maria Beadnell, of his failed marriage, and of his tormented affair with Ellen Ternan to conclude that Dickens had little direct experience of a harmonious and total union between a man and a woman. The result is that he tends to suppress any explicit recognition of the force of sexual attraction. All too often his heroines are presented as disembodied angels, patient, passive, and sexless. Agnes in *David Copperfield* exemplifies all these qualities. Mary Hogarth, whom Dickens obviously idealised, may have provided a model for his unbelievably perfect heroines: her early death certainly inspired the death of Little Nell in *The Old Curiosity Shop*, a scene which modern readers find impossibly sentimental, but which drew floods of tears from the Victorian public.

Both in his childhood and in his adult life Dickens lacked the emotional security to be found in a happy family. On the positive side we may suppose that this lack of emotional security saved him from complacency and led him to identify passionately with the poor, the lonely, and the outcast. Could a secure and happy man have understood Pip and Magwitch as well as Dickens does in *Great Expectations*? On the negative side we can point to the excessive sentimentality and tearful pathos of so many scenes that embarrass the modern reader. Perhaps Dickens's own emotional needs are so great that he cannot trust the reader's response and let the situation speak for itself. All too often, when the fictional events are already striking enough to provoke a strong reaction, Dickens spoils the effect with explicit and unashamed appeals for sympathy.

Dickens and his time

We have seen that Dickens's personal experience plays a large part in shaping the world of his fiction. It would, however, be a serious mistake to read his novels primarily as a substitute for autobiography or as the revelation of his private crises and complexes. Dickens was very much a social novelist and we cannot appreciate the moral significance of his work unless we relate it to the values and structures of the society that it reflects and criticises.

Victorian England is characterised by the full development of the industrial revolution. England became the first industrial nation in the world and, by 1850, the first nation to have more people employed in industry than in agriculture. Expanding trade coincided with the growth of the Empire and brought great wealth to Britain, but this wealth was not evenly distributed. Many enterprising individuals (the 'self-made men') rose from humble origins to positions of wealth and influence, but large sections of the working class were forced into the overcrowded slums of large cities where they worked long hours for low wages in unhealthy conditions. The manufacturing towns of the north of England provided some of the worst examples and inspired such socially conscious novels as Kingsley's *Alton Locke* (1850), Mrs Gaskell's *Mary Barton* (1848), and Dickens's own *Hard Times* (1854). In the south there was London, already the largest city in the world, showing all the crime, vice, and misery that result from overpopulation and unplanned growth. The dominant economic doctrines of the time were Free Trade and *laissez faire* (French for 'don't interfere') meaning that government should not intervene in the natural processes of commerce and industry. On the one hand, such policies encouraged individual initiative and helped industrial growth: on the other hand, they often left the working class without effective protection against the abuses of uncontrolled capitalism. During the eighteen-forties, when social tension was at its highest, Benjamin Disraeli (later Conservative prime minister) wrote in his novel, *Sybil* (1845) that England consisted of two nations: the rich and the poor.

Disraeli's famous phrase was a dramatic way of stating the extremes of wealth and poverty in Victorian England, but we should not accept it uncritically. It would be quite wrong to think of Victorian society as divided rigidly into two classes. The development of trade and the general increase in national wealth led to an unprecedented increase in social mobility and created a wide variety of intermediary classes, ranging from highly skilled workers and artisans to shopkeepers, merchants, professional men, and small capitalists. It was these middle classes who provided most of the characters in the novels of Dickens and who constituted the novelist's most faithful audience. It was also the middle classes who provided most of the energy for philanthropy and reform in the nineteenth century. The philanthropic effort created an amazing number of private bodies concerned with poor relief, popular education, medical care, and moral improvement. The movements for reform produced an impressive list of political achievements. The Reform Bills of 1832 and 1867 made Parliament a more democratic body, and the Factory Acts limited working hours, restricted child labour, and imposed safety regulations. Other reforms included prison reform, a softening of the harsher legal punishments, the gradual legalisation of trade unions, and the establishment of compulsory elementary education.

Dickens was, without question, a spokesman for the reforming conscience of the middle classes. On an immediate practical level he was involved in a number of philanthropic ventures and supported the Administrative Reform Association. But it was his novels that really played a leading part in awakening the public conscience to social evils. *Oliver Twist* shows the brutality of the obsolete laws for poor relief and exposes the vice and crime of the London underworld: *David Copperfield* and *Nicholas Nickleby* present the callous exploitation of pupils in private boarding schools: *Hard Times* portrays the dehumanising effects of industry on both capitalist and worker: *Bleak House* attacks the contagious and disheartening inefficiency of the civil law: *Little Dorrit* satirises public bureaucracy and reveals the corruption of high finance.

It is not surprising that Dickens has sometimes been called the greatest reformer in Victorian England. And yet we must be careful not to simplify the complex relationship between a writer and his public. Like so many great writers, Dickens both reflects and creates the conscience of his time, and it is, therefore, impossible to measure his practical effect in modifying Victorian attitudes and institutions. The movement for reform would surely have progressed even without the help of his immense talent. Nevertheless, it is to the credit of Dickens that he chose to speak for a new social conscience and, in doing so, accelerated the advance of reform. The vast public certainly believed that the work of Dickens produced practical results. Among the many tributes he received, perhaps the most sincere and significant came on the day of his funeral from a humble cabman who remarked 'we cabmen were always hoping he would do a turn for us one day'.

The recognition of Dickens as a social reformer should not lead us to think of him as a politically committed novelist. Individual readers may draw political conclusions from his portrayal of Victorian society, but Dickens himself never suggested that England's problems could be solved by any particular political doctrine. He may criticise Parliament, the courts, the education system, or the evils of irresponsible capitalism, but he never explicitly suggests how such things could be reformed or what could be put in their place. As George Orwell has said, 'Dickens's criticism of society is almost exclusively moral ... There is no clear sign that he wants the existing order to be overthrown, or that he believes it would make very much difference if it *were* overthrown'.* It seems that Dickens, like most Englishmen, distrusted political ideologies or, indeed, any attempt to impose an official order on the vital processes of social life. In the long run, he believed in a change of heart, not a change of system; a moral revolution, not a political one. This, of course, did not stop him from supporting specific reforms and it does not stop his readers from concluding that there was something radically wrong with the system. But the real function of Dickens's social criticism is to expose evils and arouse the public conscience. Beyond that he does not care to venture.

Thus it can be said that Dickens accepts the social and economic structures of his time while fighting for more humane attitudes that would modify their ill effects. In this he reflects the view of his middle-class readers. Despite Dickens's sympathy for the working poor, he is essentially a middle-class novelist. It is significant that, in most of his novels (*Oliver Twist, Nicholas Nickleby, David Copperfield, Great*

*George Orwell, 'Charles Dickens' in *Decline of the English Murder and Other Essays*, Penguin Books, Harmondsworth, 1965, p.83.

Expectations), the hero is rewarded with middle-class security and wealth, and this happy ending is usually brought about by individual acts of generosity and compassion. The answer to social injustice is the good rich man.

In conclusion, we should remember that Dickens does not give a totally pessimistic picture of life in Victorian England. In the early works especially there is an exuberance that is very near to optimism. He may have been horrified by the slums of London, but he loved the excitement and bustle of a large city. If we exclude sex, the novels of Dickens can be seen to contain an astonishing catalogue of human pleasures. He describes, with obvious relish, the joys of eating, drinking, smoking, talking, walking, rowing, riding in a stagecoach, or going to the theatre. Above all, he takes delight in the immense variety of human types, physical, mental, social, and professional. The Victorian world that Dickens presents contains shocking poverty and injustice, but it remains exhilarating in its abundance, diversity, and sheer vitality. In seeing Dickens as a social reformer, we should not forget that he is also a great comic novelist. There is no necessary contradiction between these two achievements.

Dickens and his public

Dickens is the most popular novelist that England has ever known. During his lifetime some of his novels reached a circulation of a hundred thousand copies, figures that would make him a bestseller even by modern standards. This popularity has never declined. In the century that has passed since the death of Dickens his novels have reached millions of readers all over the world, making him the most widely-read English author after Shakespeare. Today the audience for Dickens is still expanding through adaptations for television, cinema, and the theatre. The fictional world of Dickens has become thoroughly integrated into popular culture. Oliver Twist, Micawber, Uriah Heep, Tiny Tim, Squeers, Scrooge, and dozens of other characters are part of English folklore. Wherever English is spoken, the adjective 'Dickensian' conjures up a world of images.

One reason for the popularity of Dickens can be sought in what we call his 'mode of production'. All his novels were published in serial form, appearing regularly in weekly or monthly instalments. The interval between composition and publication was so short that Dickens never completed a novel before it began to appear in serial form. Serialisation prevented Dickens from seriously revising his work, and, especially in the early novels, led to loose episodic structure. It had, however, the immense advantage of bringing the writer close to his public since he could respond to popular opinion as his novel proceeded. It is, in fact, easy to see how Dickens manufactures climaxes and introduces new characters in order to maintain the interest of his readers. Kathleen Tillotson has compared this situation to 'the stimulating contact which an actor or public speaker receives from an audience'.* To this we might add that serialisation allows the public no interval in which to forget the author or find new favourites. For three decades Dickens kept his audience supplied with a constant flow of fiction.

There are, of course, more profound reasons for the lasting popularity of Dickens. His relationship with the public depended upon a genuine communion of feeling. He did not need to flatter public taste or debase his art for the sake of popularity. Dickens and his readers shared the same taste. An episode like the death of Little Nell drew tears not only from the audience, but also from Dickens himself. The Victorian public was, on the whole, sentimental, moralistic, and pragmatic. Dickens shared all these qualities, holding that it is good for men to laugh and weep, believing in simple non-sectarian religious values, indifferent or hostile to intellectual theories.

Dickens was not a highly-cultured man. He knew the English novelists and he idolised Shakespeare, but he was in no sense an intellectual. His novels contain no significant reference to music, the fine arts, theology, or philosophy. Sophisticated readers have often accused Dickens of being simple-minded and vulgar, yet it is one of his strengths that he speaks without condescension. He may preach, but he does not lecture: and what he preaches is not some fashionable or complex intellectual theory, but the basic moral values that he shares with the common reader.

A note on the setting

The story of *Great Expectations* is set in Kent and London and covers roughly the two decades between 1810 and 1830. Pip's village is situated somewhere on the flat land between the Thames Estuary and the mouth of the River Medway. The Hulks were old ships used as temporary prisons for convicts awaiting transportation to Australia. Until 1835 transported convicts could be sentenced to death if they returned to England without permission, although, in fact, nobody was hanged for this offence after 1810. Transportation of convicts was abolished in 1852.

*Kathleen Tillotson, *Novels of the Eighteen-Forties*, Clarendon Press, Oxford, 1954, p.36 (Later issued by Oxford University Press, London, 1961).

A note on the text

In October 1860 Dickens was worried by the falling sales of his periodical, *All the Year Round*, which was serialising an inferior novel by Charles Lever (1806–72), the Irish novelist. Dickens decided to remedy the situation by starting a novel of his own to be called *Great Expectations*. From December 1860 to June 1861 it appeared in weekly instalments on the front page of *All the Year Round* while sales improved as Dickens had hoped. In October 1861 it was published in three volumes by Chapman and Hall of London.

In his original ending to the novel Dickens made Pip and Estella meet by chance in a London street. They greet each other politely and then separate, although Pip realises that suffering has 'given her a heart to understand what my heart used to be'. The novelist Edward Bulwer Lytton (1803–73) found this ending too pessimistic and persuaded Dickens to change it. The revised ending concludes with the phrase 'I saw no shadow of another parting from her' which allows us to suppose that Pip and Estella will be married. There is much debate about which of the two endings is preferable. The revised ending is always published as representing the author's final decision, but most good modern editions include the original version in an appendix.

Among the early editions of Dickens we should note the Library Edition (30 volumes, 1861–74) and the Charles Dickens Edition (21 volumes, 1867–74). The text of *Great Expectations* in the Charles Dickens Edition contains some minor revisions of the 1861 version, mostly involving spelling and punctuation. The standard modern edition of Dickens is the New Oxford Illustrated Dickens (21 volumes, Oxford University Press, London, 1947–59), though this is gradually being superseded by the Clarendon Dickens which began in 1966. The text recommended to readers of these Notes is *Great Expectations*, edited by Angus Calder (Penguin English Library, Penguin Books, Harmondsworth, 1965).

Part 2

Summaries
of GREAT EXPECTATIONS

A general summary

Pip, an orphan, lives with his shrewish sister and her good-natured husband, the blacksmith Joe Gargery. One winter evening an escaped convict, Magwitch, frightens Pip into stealing a file and some food from the forge. While fighting on the marshes with another convict, Magwitch is recaptured. Shortly after this, Pip is invited to play at Satis House, home of the wealthy Miss Havisham, who has lived in seclusion since she was abandoned on her wedding day. Here he meets Estella, a beautiful girl who treats him with contempt. The visits stop when Miss Havisham pays for Pip to become Joe's apprentice. Mrs Joe is paralysed by a blow from a leg-iron and Pip suspects Orlick, Joe's surly journey-man. Pip's friend Biddy comes to the forge as housekeeper, but Pip is still in love with Estella and dissatisfied with his humble condition. His life is changed when Jaggers, a London lawyer, tells him that a mysterious benefactor has provided money to make him a gentleman with 'great expectations'. Pip assumes that his benefactor is Miss Havisham and already begins to behave like a snob.

Pip moves to London where, at first, he is depressed by the criminal atmosphere of Jaggers's office. He makes friends with Wemmick, Jaggers's eccentric clerk, and also with Herbert Pocket, a relative of Miss Havisham. Joe's visit to London is a failure because Pip is embarrassed by the blacksmith's awkward manners. Pip's increasing snobbery leads him to neglect Joe and Biddy. Estella comes to London and distresses Pip by flirting with the brutal Bentley Drummle. Miss Havisham is using Estella to take revenge on the male sex, but Pip still believes that Estella will be his wife. Pip secretly arranges to buy Herbert a partnership in a shipping firm. Pip's life of wealthy idleness is upset when Magwitch returns from Australia where he had been transported as a convict. Magwitch has made a fortune and he reveals himself as Pip's mysterious benefactor.

Pip is shocked to learn that Estella is to marry Drummle, but he turns his attention to Magwitch who will be hanged if he is caught in England. Pip does not want Magwitch's money. With Herbert's help, he hopes to save the convict by sending him abroad. The situation is complicated by the activities of Compeyson, a smooth criminal who once got himself a light sentence by giving false evidence against Magwitch. Compeyson was the second convict on the marshes and was also the lover who betrayed Miss Havisham. Pip visits Miss Havisham who asks his forgiveness and promises to help Herbert. That evening she gets badly burnt when her dress catches fire. Shortly after, she dies. Compeyson plots against Pip and Magwitch, finding an accomplice in Orlick who nearly succeeds in murdering Pip. At last Pip and his friends try to put Magwitch on a ship that will take him abroad. Unfortunately, they are intercepted by a police boat with Compeyson on board. In a confused struggle Compeyson is drowned and Magwitch badly wounded. Magwitch is sentenced to death, but dies in prison. Pip has discovered that Magwitch is Estella's father, and he comforts the convict's last moments by telling him that his daughter is still alive and that he (Pip) loves her. Pip falls ill and is nursed back to health by Joe whom he now recognises as a 'gentle Christian man'. He returns to his village with the idea of proposing marriage to Biddy, and finds her already married to Joe. After eleven years working with Herbert's firm in the East, Pip comes home to England as a fairly wealthy man. In the ruined garden of Satis House he meets Estella who is now a widow. The novel ends with the prospect of their marriage.

Detailed summaries

Chapter 1

In the bleak churchyard Pip weeps as he looks at the graves of his parents and brothers. He is interrupted by a convict wearing a leg-iron. On learning that Pip lives with the local blacksmith, the convict orders him to bring a file and some food to the marshes the next morning. He threatens Pip with a mysterious young man who will eat his heart and liver if he disobeys.

NOTES AND GLOSSARY
Pip searches for his own identity in the long sentence beginning 'At such a time I found out for certain ' and ending with his own name. Pip feels threatened by the landscape and sees the sea as a 'savage lair' from which the wind comes to attack him. The threat takes human form in the convict who has the marks of landscape all over his body. The gibbet suggests a danger hanging over Pip's future.

wittles:	slang for 'victuals', food
Battery:	a ruined artillery emplacement

Chapter 2

At home Pip faces the anger of his sister, but is protected by Joe. When he quickly hides some bread for the convict, Joe thinks he has been 'bolting'. Mrs Joe makes both Pip and Joe drink repulsive tar-water. Firing from the Hulks announces the escape of another convict. Pip passes a disturbed night thinking of the murderous young man and the gibbet. At dawn he steals more food and a file, and goes to meet the convict.

NOTES AND GLOSSARY
Suspense is blended with comedy in the 'bolting' scene. Mrs Joe's lack of motherly feelings is suggested by the pins and needles at her breast. The phrase 'bring up by hand' ironically suggests the violence of Mrs Joe's educational methods. Pip's own fears for the future are confirmed when Mrs Joe tells him that people who ask questions end up in the Hulks.

bolting:	swallowing without chewing
tar-water:	a disinfectant mixture of water and wood-tar
copper-stick:	used for stirring clothes in the 'copper' or washing-bowl
Hulks:	old ships used as temporary prisons
Spanish-liquorice-water:	a mild drink, not intoxicating

Chapter 3

Pip meets another convict in the fog and escapes from him, assuming that he must be the murderous young man. The first convict is waiting for Pip and devours the food with animal relish. Pip's fear of him is mixed with pity. When Pip says that he has seen the young man, the convict gets excited and begins to work on his leg-iron with the file. Pip runs home.

NOTES AND GLOSSARY
The convict has obviously invented the young man to frighten Pip. His violent reaction when he hears of the second convict suggests a mysterious connection between the two men. Notice the politeness of Pip's conversation with the convict: it is an attempt to normalise an abnormal situation, but also, perhaps, a recognition of the convict as a fellow human being.

rimy:	frosty

Chapter 4

Dressed with uncomfortable respectability, Pip and Joe go to church for Christmas. At the forge there is an abundant dinner attended by the Hubbles, Wopsle, and the pompous Uncle Pumblechook. Pip becomes the victim of the conversation when Wopsle and Pumblechook speak about the depravity of youth. Pip feels guilty and is terrified that his theft will be discovered. Pumblechook drinks the tar-water that Pip has substituted for the stolen brandy. When Pumblechook asks for the pork pie (also stolen), Pip runs for the door and is met by a soldier holding a pair of handcuffs.

NOTES AND GLOSSARY

Joe's awkwardness in his Sunday clothes demonstrates the absurdity of social pretentions. The conversation of Wopsle and Pumblechook is not only pretentious but cruel as well. When Pip is compared to a pig, we are reminded of the mysterious young man's cannibalistic designs. Joe is the only adult who shows any feeling for Pip. The whole chapter is both comic and dramatic. It ends on a note of suspense which reminds us that Dickens was writing for serial publication.

monumental Crusaders:	it was thought that in English churches the effigies of crusaders had crossed legs
penitentials:	clothes worn to show 'penitence' or sorrow for sin: Pip may also be thinking of 'penitentiary' or prison
Reformatory:	juvenile prison
banns:	announcement of marriage
thrown open:	Wopsle cannot become a clergyman in the Church of England because that profession has not been 'thrown open' to the lower classes
Squeaker:	pig
Medium:	according to Spiritualist beliefs, a medium could invoke spiritual energies to move physical objects such as a table

Chapters 5–6

Joe is asked to repair the broken handcuffs. Pumblechook and the sergeant drink the wine that Pumblechook had brought as a present to Mrs Joe. Joe, Pip, and Wopsle follow the soldiers in their search for the convicts who are eventually found fighting in the mud. Pip's convict has prevented the other from escaping. Before being taken to the Hulks, he admits that he has stolen food from the forge. Pip decides not to tell

Joe about his own part in the theft. Wopsle and Pumblechook have an argument about how the convict broke in. Pip goes to bed.

NOTES AND GLOSSARY

There is a sharp contrast between the convivial warmth of the forge and the misery of the convicts on the cold marshes. Our curiosity about the convicts is aroused when one of them is called a 'gentleman'. We see Joe's humanity when he recognises Pip's convict as a 'poor miserable fellow-creatur'. Pip's decision not to confide in Joe is the first sign of a break between them.

Hob and nob: a conventional toast
miniature windmill, sluice-gate: devices for draining the marshes and preventing floods

---

Chapter 7

While waiting to become Joe's apprentice, Pip attends the absurd evening-school kept by Wopsle's great-aunt. When he attempts to write a letter, he is surprised that Joe cannot read. Joe explains his lack of education and his submission to Mrs Joe by describing his own childhood with a drunken brutal father and a suffering mother. Uncle Pumblechook announces that Pip has been invited to play at the house of Miss Havisham, a rich recluse who lives in town. Pip is scrubbed, dressed, and sent off with Pumblechook.

NOTES AND GLOSSARY

We sympathise with Pip when we see the monotony of his life and the wretchedness of his education. Joe's apparent weakness results from genuine moral sensitivity. Pumblechook and Mrs Joe foreshadow Pip's later mistake when they think that Miss Havisham will make 'this boy's fortune'.

Catechism: a book of questions and answers about Christian beliefs
National Debt: money owed by the State to private individuals, a great sum
Mark Antony's oration: in Shakespeare's *Julius Caesar*, Act III, Scene 2
Collins: William Collins (1721–59), English poet
purple leptic: Joe's version of 'apoplectic'
Lords of the Admiralty, or Treasury: ministers of the British government
back-falls: a throw in wrestling
Mooncalfs: idiots

Chapter 8

At his corn-chandler's shop Pumblechook torments Pip with arithmetic before taking him to Satis House, a gloomy mansion attached to an abandoned brewery. Estella, a beautiful girl, escorts him to Miss Havisham, a withered old woman who sits in her bridal dress in a candlelit room amid decaying finery and stopped clocks. Miss Havisham explains that her heart is broken and that she has renounced the company of men and women. Estella and Pip play cards, and Estella scorns Pip as a 'common labouring-boy' with coarse hands and thick boots. Miss Havisham enjoys pointing out Estella's beauty and pride. Alone in the brewery, Pip weeps at his humiliation and imagines he sees Miss Havisham hanging from a beam. Estella laughs in triumph at having made him weep.

NOTES AND GLOSSARY
Pip's first contact with life at a higher social level reveals an atmosphere of splendour, decay, and cruelty. We already see Miss Havisham using Estella as an agent of revenge. Pip is easily hurt because his sister's ill-treatment has made him 'morally timid and very sensitive'. His vision of the hanging figure shows his emotional disturbance and reminds us of the gibbet in Chapter 1. It is a detail that links Satis House with the world of the convicts.

smock-frocks: loose coats worn by farmworkers

beggar my neighbour: a popular card-game

knaves, Jacks: two names for the same card, but 'Jack' was a vulgar term

Chapter 9

At home Pip tells a fantastic tale about Satis House involving a velvet coach, flags, swords, and dogs who eat from a silver basket. Pumblechook confirms the account in order to avoid admitting his ignorance. Later Pip admits to Joe that the story was invented and that he has been made to feel 'common'. Joe warns him that lies will not make him less common, but Pip already sees Joe and the forge with the scornful eyes of Estella.

NOTES AND GLOSSARY
Pip's story shows an imaginative temperament and also his desire to keep Satis House and the forge separate. His new and bitter social awareness makes him deaf to the moral advice of Joe.

outdacious: Joe's version of 'audacious'

Chapter 10

The evening-school offers Pip little hope of becoming less common, though he is helped by Biddy, a distant relative of Wopsle. One evening, with Joe at the Three Jolly Bargemen, Pip meets an inquisitive stranger who stirs his drink with a file. He gives Pip a shilling wrapped in some paper which turns out to be two pound-notes.

NOTES AND GLOSSARY
The reappearance of the file and its connection with money is a clue that Pip's fortune may be connected with the convict.

Blue Blazes: a common oath
professional occasion: Wopsle's profession as church-clerk teaches him which marriages are prohibited
Richard the Third: a play by Shakespeare

Chapter 11

Pip meets Miss Havisham's sycophantic relatives who have come for her birthday. Among them is Camilla who claims to suffer in sympathy with Miss Havisham. They mention another relative, Matthew Pocket, who refuses to join them. Again Estella scorns Pip and tries to make him cry. Pip helps Miss Havisham to walk round the dining-room where a decayed wedding-cake, overrun with spiders, stands on the table where Miss Havisham will lie when she is dead. When the relatives have been dismissed, Estella and Pip play cards again while Miss Havisham comments on the girl's beauty. In the garden Pip is forced to fight by a pale youth. Pip wins easily, but the youth bears no malice. Estella allows Pip to kiss her, but he feels that it is a meaningless gesture.

NOTES AND GLOSSARY
The decayed wedding-cake is symbolic of Miss Havisham's rotten and poisonous mind. Her treatment of her relatives prepares us for the time when she will torment them by letting them think that Pip will inherit her wealth. The card game between Pip and Estella follows the pattern of Chapter 8 to suggest a sterile unchanging relationship. Note the neat contrast between the pale youth who is courteous when he fights and Estella who is insulting when she is kissed.

toadies and humbugs: flatterers and hypocrites
deep trimmings: special clothes to suggest mourning

sal volatile:	solution of ammonium carbonate used in fainting-fits
staylace:	the lace of a corset

Chapters 12–13

Pip feels guilty about his fight with the pale youth, but his visits to Satis House continue as usual. He now confides in Biddy rather than Joe. Pumblechook and Mrs Joe speculate about Pip's possible reward. Eventually, in an embarrassing interview, Miss Havisham gives Joe twenty-five guineas to pay for Pip's apprenticeship and dismisses the boy with the warning that he can expect no more. Mrs Joe's anger at not being invited to Satis House is soothed by Joe's diplomatic behaviour. Pip's indentures are signed, and there is a celebration at The Blue Boar, attended by Wopsle, the Hubbles, and Pumblechook who takes all the credit for Pip's good fortune. Pip knows that he will not be happy as Joe's apprentice.

NOTES AND GLOSSARY
Pip's irrational feeling of guilt links him obscurely with the criminal world of the convict. Notice how Dickens repeats the word 'bind' to suggest that Pip is tied to a life he despises. Miss Havisham's warning will be forgotten too easily.

Old Clem:	song to Saint Clement, the protector of blacksmiths
indentures:	legal contract of apprenticeship
Great Seal of England:	kept in a straw bag, used to validate laws in the King's name
pattens:	overshoes
premium:	initial fee paid by apprentice to his master
Rantipole:	madman
bound:	the usual term for becoming an apprentice
fired a rick:	burned a haystack, a traditional peasant protest
windfall:	unexpected sum of money
Commercials:	commercial travellers
O Lady Fair:	popular song by the Irish poet, Thomas Moore (1779–1852)

Chapters 14–15

Pip works hard, but no longer sees the forge as the 'road to manhood and independence'. He is haunted by the thought of Estella's scorn for his humble work. Pip now has little to learn from Biddy and Wopsle:

his attempts to educate Joe end in failure. Pip asks for a half-holiday to visit Miss Havisham. This arouses the envy of Joe's journeyman, Orlick, who quarrels with the interfering Mrs Joe. Joe knocks Orlick down, but grants him the half-holiday. Miss Havisham torments Pip by telling him that Estella is abroad being educated as a lady. In the evening Wopsle acts for Pip the story of George Barnwell. On their way home they meet Orlick and hear the guns signalling the escape of a convict. At the forge they find Mrs Joe crippled by a blow on the head.

NOTES AND GLOSSARY
Pip gains our sympathy with his frustrated efforts to obtain education. Joe shows genuine insight when he warns Pip that a visit to Satis House might look as if he 'expected something'. Notice how Dickens, through the story of George Barnwell and the firing of the guns, continues to suggest criminality as a part of Pip's experience.

lay-figure:	wooden figure of the human body
in sunders:	Joe's version of 'asunder' (apart)
journeyman:	qualified worker
noodles:	idiots
George Barnwell:	a play by George Lillo (1693–1739) about an apprentice who commits murder and is hanged
Newgate:	famous London prison
Bosworth Field:	where the King died in Shakespeare's *Richard III*

Chapter 16

A filed leg-iron is found beside Mrs Joe. It does not belong to the convicts who escaped that evening. Pip thinks it is the leg-iron worn by his convict years ago. He suspects Orlick or the man who stirred his drink with a file (Chapter 10), but the police fail to prove anything. Mrs Joe is now dumb and paralysed. She is very amiable towards Orlick. Her place in the household is taken by Biddy.

NOTES AND GLOSSARY
Dickens creates another mystery and suggests several possible solutions. Pip feels guilty, partly because he has unwittingly provided the criminal's weapon, but also because subconsciously he would have liked to attack Mrs Joe. By replacing Mrs Joe with Biddy, Dickens strengthens the moral appeal of the forge and leaves Pip less excuse for his dissatisfaction.

Bow Street men:	detective force, predecessors of the Metropolitan Police

Chapter 17

Pip's apprenticeship proceeds normally. He pays brief annual visits to Miss Havisham. He admires Biddy, but cannot forget Estella. One afternoon he tells Biddy that he wants to be a gentleman for Estella's sake. Biddy advises him that Estella is not worthy of his love and that he should not judge his life on her terms. Pip admits that it would be better to fall in love with Biddy, and she answers 'you never will'. Pip is annoyed to see that Orlick is attracted to Biddy. Pip's good resolutions for the future are frustrated by the lingering hope that Miss Havisham will make his fortune.

NOTES AND GLOSSARY
This is a chapter of subtle psychological insight. Pip, so sensitive on his own account, is highly insensitive towards Biddy whom he patronises by assuming that she would accept him as a husband. Biddy, indeed, may be in love with him, and this makes his behaviour even more tactless. Pip's violent gestures reveal his immaturity. Biddy, however, can master her emotions. She may love Pip, but she sees his faults and defends herself with dignity. Biddy's realism contrasts with Pip's attitude towards Estella. Since Pip cannot see Estella as a real person, he associates her with the prospect, and we should note that 'prospect' means both landscape and expectation.

keep company: to court with a view to marriage
I'm jiggered: a meaningless oath

Chapter 18

In the fourth year of Pip's apprenticeship a stranger comes to The Three Jolly Bargemen and humiliates Wopsle with bullying legal manners. The stranger is Jaggers, a London lawyer, who announces that Pip has inherited 'great expectations' from a mysterious benefactor. He will now leave the forge and be educated as a gentleman. Pip is warned that he must not seek to know the name of the benefactor, but he assumes that it must be Miss Havisham. He remembers seeing Jaggers at Satis House and notes that his tutor is to be Matthew Pocket (Chapter 11). Joe refuses to accept compensation for the loss of his apprentice. Pip resents the touch of sadness in the congratulations of Joe and Biddy. As he goes to bed, he is surprised that his good fortune makes him feel lonely.

NOTES AND GLOSSARY

The hero will keep his nickname of Pip: this reminds us that there will be a continuity between the apprentice and the gentleman. Circumstantial evidence convinces Pip that Miss Havisham is his benefactor, but Jaggers warns us that we have no authority for this opinion. Pip's 'division of mind' is shown by rapid changes in mood: from elation he passes to resentment ('I felt offended') and condescension ('handsomely forgiving her'), ending with nostalgia and loneliness.

cross-examined: questioned in court
well and truly try: the official oath sworn by a jury
Brag is a good dog: a proverb meaning that silence is better than speech
guardian: legal substitute for father
ekervally: Joe's version of 'equally'

Chapter 19

Pip takes a last walk on the marshes, dismissing the memory of the convict and planning generous condescension towards the villagers. He asks Biddy to improve Joe's manners in order to fit him for a 'higher sphere'. When Biddy answers that Joe has his own pride, Pip accuses her of envy. He is received deferentially by Trabb the tailor, but humiliated by Trabb's boy. Over a huge meal Pumblechook pays him exaggerated compliments, hoping that Pip will invest in his business. Miss Havisham uses Pip's good fortune to torment Sarah Pocket. Not wanting to be seen with Joe, Pip leaves for London alone. On the coach he is seized with remorse.

NOTES AND GLOSSARY

Pip behaves like a snob and we are glad to see him humiliated by Trabb's boy. The dignity of Joe and Biddy contrasts with the behaviour of Trabb, Pumblechook, and even Miss Havisham who all hope to use Pip's good fortune for their own ends. The last phrase of the chapter, 'the world lay spread before me' is almost a quotation from Milton's poem, *Paradise Lost*. It may suggest that Pip is losing his innocence and entering a world of sin.

the rich man and the Kingdom of Heaven: Christ said that it was easier for a camel to pass through the eye of a needle than for a rich man to enter Heaven (Matthew, XIX: 24)
oncommon plump: suddenly
Mother Hubbard's dog: in the nursery rhyme, Mother Hubbard goes to many shops to buy clothes for her dog

sleeping partner: one who shares the profits of a firm but takes no active part in running it.
flip: a hot alcoholic drink
old shoe: traditional symbol of good luck

Chapter 20

Pip arrives in London and is kept waiting in Jaggers's sordid office. Among the strange relics are two dreadful plaster casts (the death-masks of hanged men). Pip walks past Newgate Prison and gets 'a sickening idea of London'. At last, Jaggers arrives and Pip watches him terrorise his criminal clients. After refusing a potential witness for a trial, Jaggers tells Pip about the financial arrangements for his future and sends him off to spend the weekend with Herbert Pocket at Barnard's Inn.

NOTES AND GLOSSARY
This is an anti-climax after Pip's dreams. London is ugly, and Jaggers treats him without ceremony. We see that Jaggers will defend even the worst cause as long as he can keep within the letter of the law. We can no longer have romantic ideas about Pip's 'great expectations' when we see them connected with this corrupt atmosphere.

Little Britain: street near St Paul's Cathedral, London
minister of justice: ironic term for the gatekeeper at Newgate Prison
Cag-Maggerth: useless: 'cag-mag' is slang for bad meat
toss-up: an even chance, as in tossing a coin
Cock Robin: a nursery rhyme
Barnard's Inn: the Inns of Chancery were originally institutions for the study and practice of law. In *Great Expectations* Barnard's Inn is no longer used for this purpose
outrunning the constable: spending too much

Chapters 21–2

Pip is accompanied to Barnard's Inn by Jaggers's clerk, Wemmick, whose profession seems reflected in his dry manners and mechanical appearance. Barnard's Inn is a depressing place. Pip meets Herbert and recognises the pale youth he fought at Satis House (Chapter 11). Herbert calls Pip 'Handel' after the musician who composed 'The Harmonious Blacksmith', and tactfully corrects his table manners. He explains that he was taken to Satis House as a possible fiancé for Estella, but is glad to have escaped from this cruel girl who was adopted by Miss Havisham to 'wreak revenge on the male sex'. He then tells Pip the story of Miss Havisham. Miss Havisham, daughter of a wealthy brewer, had a half-brother who lived an extravagant wasteful life. His father disinherited him, but later relented and left him well-off, though not as rich as Miss Havisham. Once again the brother got into debt, and now he accused Miss Havisham of turning his father against him. Miss Havisham fell in love with a showy man who got large sums of money from her. Only Matthew Pocket, Herbert's father, warned her that her lover was no true gentleman. Miss Havisham dismissed Matthew who has never returned to Satis House. On the wedding morning, Miss Havisham's lover abandoned her. Since then she has never seen daylight and has let Satis House go to ruin. It was supposed that Miss Havisham's lover acted in conspiracy with her half-brother. Both men later fell into deeper shame and ruin. Finally, Pip learns about Herbert's unpaid job in a counting-house and his hopes of making a fortune in overseas trade. At the end of the chapter Pip visits the home of Matthew Pocket.

NOTES AND GLOSSARY

Herbert's story creates new mysteries. Who are Estella's real parents? What has happened to Miss Havisham's lover and her half-brother? We are also reminded of the need to distinguish between appearance and reality in defining a gentleman. Herbert himself, with his friendliness and tact, offers an example of what a gentleman should be.

a Tartar:	fierce, difficult to deal with
Lord Mayor's Feast:	annual banquet in London
a crack thing:	a respectable profession
the City:	the financial and banking district of London
'Change:	the Royal Exchange, London, centre for marine insurance

---

Chapters 23–4

The Pockets have a large disorganised household. Mr Pocket is a cultured gentleman who received a good education but now makes a poor living by tutoring. Mrs Pocket, daughter of a knight, is so absurdly concerned with social status that she is inefficient as wife and mother. The servants, Flopson and Millers, assert their independence amid the chaos. Pip goes rowing with his fellow-students, Startop and Drummle. Drummle is surly and brutish. Pip benefits from Matthew Pocket's teaching. He decides to live with Herbert at Barnard's Inn and gets money from Jaggers to buy furniture. Wemmick praises Jaggers's professional skill and takes Pip to see him dominating the courtroom. Wemmick also shows Pip the curious 'portable property' he receives as gifts from condemned criminals. After inviting Pip to his own home, he mentions that if Pip ever dines with Jaggers, he will see 'a wild beast tamed'.

NOTES AND GLOSSARY

The Pocket family provides a comic interlude. Mrs Pocket's social pretension is a caricature of Pip's own snobbery. This light scene is followed by the macabre comedy of Wemmick's 'portable property'. We see more evidence of Jaggers's power and a more human side to the mechanical Wemmick.

Baronet	hereditary title, one grade higher than Knight
mount to the Woolsack:	become Chancellor of the Exchequer (Minister of Finance)
Grinder:	private teacher of rich children
blades:	young men, with a pun on knife-blades that are sharpened by grinding
Dying Gladiator:	a famous classical sculpture
the Bailey:	the Old Bailey, a famous London court

Chapters 25–6

Pip's dislike of Drummle is confirmed. The other Pockets (Chapter 11) turn up and treat Pip with fawning hypocrisy. Pip goes to Wemmick's home, a small cottage adapted to look like a Gothic castle. Pip is touched by Wemmick's warm hospitality and by his affection for the Aged Parent who is deaf. Pip, Herbert, Startop, and Drummle are invited by Jaggers who forces his housekeeper (the 'wild beast tamed') to show them her strong wrists, one of which is deeply scarred. Drummle behaves badly, but Jaggers prevents a fight. He shows a strange interest in Drummle and warns Pip to avoid him.

NOTES AND GLOSSARY

Wemmick lives a double life: a legal machine at the office and a charming eccentric at home. His kindness to the Aged Parent contrasts with Pip's treatment of Joe. The warm atmosphere at Wemmick's also contrasts with the tension at Jaggers's dinner party. The housekeeper, Molly, adds another mystery to the plot. Jaggers's interest in Drummle suggests that he has recognised a criminal type. Notice how Jaggers washes his hands. It implies that he recognises the immorality of his profession and wants to avoid responsibility.

cracksmen:	burglars
Britannia metal:	a cheap substitute for silver
Walworth:	in *Great Expectations* still a village, now part of London
Greenwich time:	standard British time is calculated from the meridian at Greenwich
dumb-waiter:	arrangement of revolving trays for serving food and drink
Witches' caldron:	in Shakespeare's *Macbeth*

Chapter 27

A letter from Biddy announces the arrival of Joe. Pip is worried about Joe's manners and sends his servant away to avoid embarrassment. Joe brings the news (which Biddy refused to write) that Estella has returned and would like to see Pip. We also learn that Wopsle has come to London to try his fortune as an actor. Joe's visit is not a success. Pip behaves in a stiff, unnatural fashion, and Joe, though he is comically awkward, has too much dignity to remain where he is not wanted. As Joe leaves, Pip runs after him, but it is too late.

NOTES AND GLOSSARY
Biddy's refusal to write about Estella suggests that she still loves Pip. Joe is absurd when he tries to behave like a gentleman, but achieves 'simple dignity' when he speaks as a blacksmith. Pip's late reaction repeats his behaviour at the end of Chapter 19.

Roscian:	like Roscius, a famous Roman actor
National Bard:	Shakespeare
Miss A:	Joe does not pronounce the 'h' in Havisham
meshes:	slang for 'marshes'

Chapter 28

On his way to Satis House, Pip overhears a conversation between two guarded convicts. One of them is the man with the file (Chapter 10) who recalls how a fellow-convict once gave him two pounds to deliver to a boy on the marshes. On his arrival at the Blue Boar, Pip finds a newspaper article presenting Pumblechook as the friend of his youth and founder of his fortunes.

NOTES AND GLOSSARY

It is significant that Dickens reminds us of the convict just when Pip's future seems assured.

Lifer:	sentenced to prison or transportation for life
Mentor:	the advisor of Telemachus, son of Odysseus, in Homer's *Odyssey*
Quintin Matsys:	Flemish painter (1466–1530), supposedly worked as a blacksmith
Verb. Sap:	(*Latin*) *Verbum satis sapienti*, a word is enough for the wise

Chapter 29

Pip believes Miss Havisham has chosen him for Estella, whom he loves with romantic passion, despite her faults. At Satis House he finds Orlick, armed with a gun, acting as porter. Estella, more beautiful than ever, walks with Pip in the old garden. Pip has painful memories, but Estella, apparently unmoved, warns him that she has no heart. Alone with Pip, Miss Havisham urges him to love Estella with 'utter submission'. Jaggers arrives, but gives Pip no clue about Estella's parents. At dinner Jaggers torments Sarah Pocket by speaking of Pip's expectations. Seeing Jaggers and Estella together, Pip feels the contrast between the lawyer's coldness and his own passionate emotions. Back at the Blue Boar, while Pip surrenders to a rapture of love, we are reminded that he has neglected to visit Joe.

NOTES AND GLOSSARY

Pip's romantic vocabulary contrasts with his real humiliating situation. Estella's warning that she has no heart may be paradoxical since it suggests she has heart enough to feel sorry for Pip. There is an explicit connection between Pip's love for Estella and his neglect of Joe.

Chapters 30–1

After persuading Jaggers to dismiss Orlick, Pip walks through the town and is mercilessly mocked by Trabb's boy. He writes a letter of complaint to Trabb. Instead of visiting Joe, he sends him a present of codfish and oysters. Back at Barnard's Inn he tells Herbert of his love for Estella. Herbert thinks Estella may not be destined for Pip, and, even if she were, she could not make him happy. Herbert himself loves Clara, the poor daughter of a retired ship's purser. Despite a visit to Wopsle's hilarious performance of *Hamlet*, Pip is depressed.

NOTES AND GLOSSARY

Condescension to Joe and mean revenge on Trabb's boy show the depths of Pip's snobbery. Herbert shares his father's honesty (Chapter 22) when he warns Pip against Estella. His own love for the humble Clara contrasts with Pip's snobbish infatuation. Wopsle's *Hamlet* provides splendid comic relief.

gift-horse:	proverb, 'Never look a gift-horse in the mouth', don't be critical of what is freely given
sour grapes:	in the Greek fables of Aesop (*c*620–*c*560BC), the fox consoles himself for the loss of the grapes by pretending they were sour

---

Chapters 32–3

A note from Estella announces her visit to London. While Pip waits for her, he is taken by Wemmick to Newgate Prison where the clerk conducts routine business and takes farewell of a man condemned to death. Pip feels the contrast between this sordid atmosphere and Estella's beauty. He wonders why he is surrounded with the taint of crime. When he sees Estella, a 'nameless shadow' crosses his mind. Estella is to live with a family in Richmond who will introduce her to society. She warns Pip against the conspiring Pockets whom she loves to torment, and enquires briefly about Newgate and Jaggers whom she obviously dislikes. Her behaviour towards Pip is like that of someone obeying orders. Pip accompanies her to Richmond.

NOTES AND GLOSSARY

We are prepared for future revelations by the 'nameless shadow' and by the connection of Estella with Newgate. Her behaviour suggests that she and Pip are 'mere puppets' controlled by others. Notice how Dickens blends serious conversation with comic observations on the service at the inn.

beat:	a watchman's round, a habitual walk
taking a squint:	slang for 'looking at'
quantum:	sufficient sum
pigeon-fancier:	breeder or trainer of racing-pigeons
Coiner:	forger
manslaughter:	a less serious charge than murder
Moses in the bullrushes:	the Bible tells how Moses was found in the bullrushes by the Pharaoh's daughter (Exodus II: 3–6)

| **Farthingale:** | hooped female dress in seventeenth and eighteenth centuries |

Chapter 34

Pip lives an idle life, disturbed by guilt towards Joe and Biddy. His expensive habits are copied by Herbert whose prospects have not improved. Pip and Herbert join a foolish club called 'The Finches of the Grove'. Drummle is one of the members. One evening, when they are calculating their debts, Pip and Herbert hear that Mrs Joe has died.

NOTES AND GLOSSARY
Pip's way of life has no real purpose. He makes a poor return for friendship by leading Herbert into expensive habits.

| **canary-breasted:** | yellow-coated |
| **Covent Garden:** | at that time a disreputable area of London |

Chapter 35

Although Pip has never loved his sister, her death shocks him and reminds him of her unknown attacker. The funeral is a pompous farce, spoiled by Pumblechook's insensitivity, except for the final moments when Mrs Joe is buried amid the peaceful landscape. Biddy, who intends to teach in the new school, recounts the death of Mrs Joe whose last words were 'Joe', 'pardon', and 'Pip'. Biddy is still being followed by Orlick who now works in the quarries. Pip promises to come to the forge more often and is angry when Biddy doubts his word.

NOTES AND GLOSSARY
Dickens intensifies moments of great pathos by setting them against a background of broad humour and social satire. The conversation between Pip and Biddy suggests a relationship that has reached break-ing-point. From now on Biddy will no longer be available as an alternative to Estella.

| **mummery:** | play-acting |

Chapters 36–7

On Pip's twenty-first birthday Jaggers tells him that he will have an annual income of five hundred pounds, but refuses to answer any questions about the mysterious benefactor. Pip asks Wemmick how to help Herbert's career. Wemmick's official view is that Pip would be throwing his money away. In the relaxed atmosphere of his home, however, Wemmick takes a more human approach and arranges for Pip to buy Herbert a partnership with Clarriker, a shipping-broker. The arrangements are secret, but Pip enjoys seeing Herbert's new optimism. Pip is amused by Wemmick's mechanical courting of Miss Skiffins.

NOTES AND GLOSSARY
Pip himself becomes an anonymous benefactor, a good deed that will have important consequences. Wemmick's hospitable home is a partial substitute for the forge in Pip's London life.

Union Jack:	national flag of Great Britain
Wine-Coopering:	making barrels for wine
jorum:	large drinking-bowl, metaphorically a large amount
powder-mill:	explosives factory

Chapter 38

Pip often sees Estella at Richmond where he is made jealous by her other suitors. She still warns him not to love her. On a visit to Satis House, Pip hears Miss Havisham rejoice in Estella's cruelty to men, but he still thinks that Estella will marry him when Miss Havisham's revenge is satisfied. Miss Havisham accuses Estella of being cold towards her: Estella replies that Miss Havisham taught her to be heartless. That night Pip sees Miss Havisham wandering round the house in distress. At the Finches Club Drummle claims to know Estella. When Estella confirms this, Pip reproaches her for favouring a boor. Estella answers that she deceives Drummle and everyone else except Pip. We are prepared for the next chapter with the story of a heavy slab slowly prepared to fall on a Sultan in the moment of his conquest.

NOTES AND GLOSSARY
Miss Havisham is caught in her own trap. She taught Estella to be cruel and now that cruelty turns against her. Pip deceives himself. Despite the evidence, he thinks he will be exempted from Miss Havisham's revenge. Notice the stiff theatrical quality of the dialogue between Estella and Miss Havisham. There is no real communication between people who are condemned to act inhuman roles.

addle-headed predecessors: stupid ancestors

Chapter 39

On a stormy night, while Herbert is away in Marseilles, Pip (now twenty-three) is visited by a stranger whom he recognises as the convict (Chapters 1–5). Pip wants to dismiss this ghost from the past, but is moved by tears in the man's eyes. He guesses that the convict once sent him two pounds (Chapter 10), but is shocked to learn that the convict, not Miss Havisham, is his mysterious benefactor. After being transported to Australia, the convict had worked hard and made a fortune which he now uses to make Pip a gentleman. Feeling like Pip's 'second father', he has returned to see the gentleman he owns. Pip realises that Miss Havisham has used his expectations as a way of tormenting her greedy relatives: Estella was never meant for him. Worst of all, it is for a guilty convict that he has neglected Joe. But the punishment for a transported convict who returns is death, and so Pip decides to shelter his unwelcome guest.

NOTES AND GLOSSARY
Dickens succeeds in dividing our sympathies between Pip and the convict. We see that Pip's idle life has been based on the convict's hard work, and we learn that an outcast may still be capable of courage, endurance, and gratitude. But gratitude is not the convict's only motive. As Miss Havisham uses Estella, so he has used Pip to take revenge on society. Pip gains our sympathy because he is partly a victim. His vices have been partly forced upon him from outside.

a game one: a lively or daring fellow
warmint: Magwitch's version of 'vermin', a repulsive animal

Chapters 40–1

To avoid suspicion, Pip announces that his uncle has arrived from the country. In the morning he stumbles over a man hiding on the staircase, and learns from the watchman that someone with dusty clothes had followed his visitor through the gate. The convict's assumed name is Provis, but his real name is Abel Magwitch. Pip is distressed by his rough manners and even more by his delight in the 'London gentleman' he has made. Jaggers confirms Magwitch's story while avoiding any formal admission that he knows the convict has returned. He denies responsibility for Pip's mistaken ideas about his benefactor. Pip disguises Magwitch as a farmer and finds him lodgings in Essex Street, but Magwitch still looks like a convict. Herbert returns and Magwitch swears him to secrecy while promising to make his fortune. Pip tells Herbert that he can no longer accept the convict's money. Herbert agrees and suggests a job with Clarriker (Chapter 37). Meanwhile they cannot risk destroying Magwitch's dream. Pip's first task must be to save Magwitch by getting him out of England. They decide to question Magwitch about his past.

NOTES AND GLOSSARY

Pip was embarrassed by Joe's visit (Chapter 27): it is ironic that now he has to present a convict as his uncle. Notice how Dickens reminds us of the main theme by repeating the word 'gentleman'. Magwitch is pathetically uncertain in his behaviour, shifting between the pride of ownership ('this is the gentleman what I made') and humble apologies for being 'low'. After his long passivity, Pip becomes a man of action who puts someone else's interest before his own.

grubber: slang for 'eater'
Botany Bay: where transported convicts disembarked in Australia
Calendar: the *Newgate Calendar* (1771) contained biographies of criminals
the imaginary student: the hero of Mary Shelley's *Frankenstein* (1818)
crib: slang for 'shelter'
shake-down: slang for 'bed'

Chapter 42

Magwitch tells his story. He never knew his parents, but he remembers being abandoned, stealing turnips, and feeling cold. His childhood was passed in and out of jail. Society offered him moral advice but no way of making a living. Thus he was forced to steal and treated as a 'hardened' criminal. He did the sort of jobs that 'don't pay and lead to trouble'. At Epsom Races he met Compeyson, a heartless criminal with the manners and education of a gentleman. Compeyson has another companion called Arthur who had once helped Compeyson to swindle a rich lady. The money was wasted in gambling, and Arthur died haunted by the vision of the lady. At last, Compeyson and Magwitch were arrested for their crimes. At the trial Compeyson blamed Magwitch and, because he seemed a gentleman, got a light sentence. Magwitch got fourteen years. Magwitch took revenge by preventing Compeyson's escape (Chapter 5). Magwitch was then transported for life and never heard what happened to Compeyson. Halfway through his story, Magwitch mentions his wife, but stops short. Herbert gives Pip a note saying that Arthur was Miss Havisham's half-brother and Compeyson her lover.

NOTES AND GLOSSARY

Magwitch emerges as a victim of society: this contrasts with Pip's earlier vision of him as 'loaded with all the crimes in the Calendar' (Chapter 40). The social theme of the novel is reinforced by the fact that Compeyson, like Pip, 'set up for a gentleman'. The injustice of the legal system is revealed by the different sentences passed on Compeyson and Magwitch. Dickens arouses our curiosity through the reference to Magwitch's wife and the mystery that still surrounds Compeyson.

Summun:	Magwitch's version of 'someone'
Traveller's Rest:	a shelter used by tramps
taturs:	slang for 'potatoes'
Epsom:	a famous racecourse
dab:	an expert
the horrors:	slang for the delirium caused by alcoholism
Missis:	slang for 'wife'
Bridewells and Lock-Ups:	prisons

Chapters 43–4

Pip realises that if Compeyson is still alive and hears of Magwitch's return, he will inform the police. Pip goes down to Satis House to see Estella. At the Blue Boar he finds Drummle, as insolent as ever. He also glimpses a man who looks like Orlick. At Satis House Miss Havisham admits that she encouraged Pip to regard her as his benefactor in order to torment the Pockets. Pip praises Matthew and Herbert Pocket and asks her to continue the secret help he gave to Herbert (Chapter 37). Turning to Estella, he declares his love. Estella replies that she does not know the meaning of love and that she will marry Drummle. This is her own decision, not Miss Havisham's. After pleading with her not to marry a brute, Pip leaves. Miss Havisham seems overcome with remorse. Pip walks back to London and finds a message from Wemmick saying 'Don't go home'.

NOTES AND GLOSSARY

Estella's marriage completes the overthrow of Pip's expectations. Pip's parting speech suggests that he has loved an imaginative creation ('the embodiment of every graceful fancy') rather than a real person. We have further proof of Pip's moral growth. Even in this crisis, he thinks first of Herbert.

Chapters 45–6

After a wretched night in the Hummums Hotel, Pip goes to Wemmick's home. Informants at Newgate have told Wemmick that Pip's apartment is being watched and that Compeyson is living in London. Herbert and Wemmick have moved Magwitch to the house of Clara Barley (Herbert's fiancée). Since the house is by the Thames, it is a good place for Magwitch to stay until he can be slipped on board a foreign ship. Pip spends a peaceful day with Wemmick's Aged Parent before going to Clara's. Clara lives with her bedridden father, Bill Barley, who can be heard cursing upstairs. At the top of the house is Magwitch who seems strangely more gentle than before. Pip and Herbert agree to start rowing on the river so that eventually they can take Magwitch to a ship without arousing suspicion. A drawn blind on Magwitch's window will be a sign that all is well. Back at Pip's lodgings, everything is quiet.

NOTES AND GLOSSARY

The threat to Magwitch grows with the news that Compeyson is still alive. Pip and Magwitch grow closer to each other as Pip accepts responsibility for the convict's safety. The tender relationship between Herbert and Clara contrasts with Pip's frustrated love for Estella. Note the comic relief provided by Bill Barley.

the Hummums: name of a hotel
rush-light: a cheap candle
Argus: in Greek mythology Argus had a hundred eyes
Double Gloucester: a celebrated English cheese
to 'shoot' the bridge: pass through the dangerous narrow arches

Chapter 47

Before trying to get Magwitch out of England, Pip waits for a sign from Wemmick. Meanwhile he rows regularly on the river. Deeply in debt, he still refuses to use Magwitch's money. One evening he goes to see Wopsle acting, not in *Hamlet*, but in a ridiculous pantomime. Afterwards Wopsle says that he saw one of the convicts from the marshes sitting behind Pip in the theatre. Pip realises that he is being followed by Compeyson and informs Wemmick.

NOTES AND GLOSSARY

Another example of comedy alternating with dramatic tension.

Swab: term of abuse among sailors

Chapter 48

At dinner with Jaggers and Wemmick, Pip receives a note that Miss Havisham wants to see him about a business matter. Jaggers speculates about Estella and Drummle, saying that Drummle will either 'beat or cringe' (act violently or submit). Observing Jaggers's housekeeper, Molly, Pip is reminded of what Estella might be after an unhappy marriage. He remembers the 'nameless shadow' of Chapter 32 and becomes convinced that Molly is Estella's mother. Later Wemmick explains that Jaggers had once defended Molly against a charge of murdering another woman. The victim was strong and Jaggers argued that Molly was too weak to have killed her. The scars on Molly's wrists could have been caused by brambles. Molly, who was also suspected of killing her child, was acquitted and became Jaggers's housekeeper.

NOTES AND GLOSSARY

It is clear that Molly is Estella's mother and that, despite her acquittal, she is a murderess. We thus have another connection between Satis House and the criminal underworld. But mysteries remain: how did Estella come to Satis House? who is her father?

winding-sheets: the wax drippings on the candle are like the shroud that wraps a corpse

won the pool: made a successful bet

couldn't work it himself: as an attorney (now called 'solicitor'), Jaggers cannot speak in the higher courts

put in all the salt and pepper: did all the effective work

over the broomstick: a way of saying that Molly was not legally married

Chapter 49

Pip goes to see Miss Havisham and is moved to pity by her loneliness. He explains how he has helped Herbert and why he cannot continue to do so. Miss Havisham arranges for Jaggers to pay the nine hundred pounds needed to complete Herbert's partnership with Clarriker. She hopes Pip will one day write 'I forgive her' under her name. Pip says that he does forgive her and that he needs forgiveness himself. Miss Havisham weeps with remorse, remembering not only Pip but also Estella, now married to Drummle. At first, she had only wanted to save Estella from misery: later, seeing her beauty, she used her for revenge. She knows nothing of Estella's parents. She had wanted a girl to love, and so Jaggers had brought Estella to Satis House at the age of two or three. As he is leaving, Pip has his old vision of Miss Havisham hanging in the brewery (Chapter 8). Turning back, he sees her dress catch fire and rushes to save her. She is seriously burned and badly shocked. The surgeon promises to inform Estella (now in Paris), and Pip agrees to contact the Pockets. He leaves Miss Havisham lying on the table (Chapter 11), deliriously muttering about remorse and forgiveness.

NOTES AND GLOSSARY
Miss Havisham's real crime is not revenge but willed isolation. This crime is its own punishment because it makes her 'unfit for the earth'. The burning wedding dress suggests symbolically that Miss Havisham is destroyed by the obsession with her own past.

Chapters 50–1

While treating Pip's burns, Herbert recounts what he has learned from Magwitch. Magwitch was once linked to a jealous woman who murdered her rival and was defended by Jaggers. The woman had also threatened to kill their daughter whom Magwitch loved deeply. Magwitch thinks that she did kill the child. During the trial he stayed hidden to avoid testifying against the woman who had shared his life. After the acquittal, he lost contact with her. Compeyson knew why Magwitch had stayed hidden and used this knowledge to blackmail him into subjection. A rapid calculation of dates convinces Pip that Magwitch is Estella's father. Pip sees Jaggers, tells him what he has learned, and asks for more information. Jaggers tries to change the subject, but is softened when Pip appeals for Wemmick's support and reveals the clerk's unsuspected home life. In a cautious legal way, Jaggers explains that when Molly's case occurred he saw a chance of saving one child from the mass of children destined to misery and destruction. He therefore sent Estella to satisfy Miss Havisham's request and kept Molly as his servant. He warns Pip not to degrade Estella by revealing her parentage. Jaggers and Wemmick seem ashamed of their own humanity. Mike (Chapter 20) gets thrown out for mentioning his feelings.

NOTES AND GLOSSARY
We see the humanity, not only of Magwitch, but also of Jaggers who once acted with compassion and had his own 'poor dreams'. The way Jaggers and Wemmick resume their normal roles is richly comic and very significant: human feelings have no place in their dehumanising profession. Estella's background has the same criminal taint as Pip's gentility. This, at least, unites them.

pegging: knocking
depose: give evidence, especially in writing

Chapter 52

Pip completes the partnership arrangements for Herbert who will soon go East to establish a branch of Clarriker's firm. One Monday in March a note from Wemmick suggests that Wednesday would be the right time for Magwitch's escape. Pip and Herbert decide to pick up Magwitch, row down on the ebb-tide, and then wait for the Hamburg steamer. Since Pip's burns prevent him from rowing, Startop will be brought in to help. Later in the day a second note tells Pip to go to the sluice-house by the lime kiln on the marshes for information about Provis (Magwitch). The anonymous note warns him to tell nobody, so he leaves a letter for Herbert saying he has gone to Satis House. After stopping at Satis House, he dines at an inn where the landlord talks about Pumblechook who has been disgracefully treated by the youth he helped. Pip thinks of the uncomplaining Joe. Setting out for the marshes, he realises he has lost the anonymous letter.

NOTES AND GLOSSARY
Once again Pip is totally concerned with other people (Herbert and Magwitch). We are reminded of Joe.

Chapter 53

At the sluice-house Pip is trapped by Orlick who carries a gun (Chapter 29). He intends to kill Pip and burn his body in the lime kiln. Orlick accuses Pip of spoiling his chances with Biddy and getting him dismissed from Satis House. Drinking heavily, he admits that he attacked Mrs Joe (Chapter 15). Now he works for Compeyson and knows all about Magwitch who will be caught and hanged when Pip is dead. It was Orlick who hid on Pip's stairs (Chapter 40). At the last moment Pip is saved by Herbert, Startop, and Trabb's boy. Orlick escapes. Herbert had found Orlick's letter in Pip's apartment. He and Startop had gone straight to Miss Havisham's: then Trabb's boy had led them to the sluice-house. They decide not to pursue Orlick whose arrest might be fatal for Magwitch. After rewarding Trabb's boy, Pip returns to London, spends Tuesday recovering, and feels ready when Wednesday dawns.

NOTES AND GLOSSARY
Orlick says Pip is partly responsible for the attack on Mrs Joe: we remember that Pip felt guilty at the time (Chapter 16). Faced by death, Pip does not worry about the loss of his expectations, only about Magwitch, Herbert, Joe and Biddy, who will think he has abandoned them. We are glad to see Trabb's boy rewarded.

farden:	a farthing, the least valuable coin
weazen:	slang for 'throat'
'ware them:	slang for 'beware of them'
nevvy:	slang for 'nephew'

Chapter 54

Herbert, Startop, and Pip pick up Magwitch at Mill Pond Bank and row downriver amid the crowded shipping. Magwitch enjoys his freedom and faces the danger with dignity. By evening they have passed Gravesend and are in a lonely part of the river. There is no sign that they have been followed. They decide to wait at a lonely inn until it is time to catch the steamer (one o'clock the following afternoon). Pip is disturbed to hear that a four-oared galley has been seen. He then spots two men inspecting his boat. Magwitch reassures him that they are probably customs officers who are not concerned with them. In the morning Pip and Magwitch walk out to a point where Herbert and Startop pick them up. At half-past one the Hamburg steamer arrives followed by another ship for Rotterdam. At the same time a four-oared galley comes up and calls on Magwitch to surrender. In a scene of great confusion, Magwitch tears the cloak from a man in the galley and reveals Compeyson. The steamer smashes Pip's boat. While struggling with Compeyson in the water, Magwitch is badly wounded by the steamer. Compeyson is drowned. Magwitch is arrested, but he is consoled by the thought that he has made Pip a gentleman. Pip does not tell him that all his money will be confiscated. Pip knows Magwitch will be condemned to death and thinks it would be better if he died of his wounds. He sees Magwitch as 'a better man than I had been to Joe' and resolves to stay by him until the end.

NOTES AND GLOSSARY
In facing danger together, Pip and Magwitch overcome the social barriers that divide them. Notice that it is Magwitch, the one who is really in danger, who tries to reassure Pip. It may be significant that the final setting is like Pip's 'own marsh country'. Perhaps, in helping the convict again (this time willingly), Pip recovers some of his childhood innocence. For further discussion of this important chapter, you should read carefully through the Commentary, Part 3.

coal-whippers:	men who unload coal from ships
ballast-lighters:	barges carrying ballast up-river to sailing-ships
thowels:	wooden pegs serving as rowlocks for the oars
jack:	odd-job man

Chapter 55

Magwitch's trial is postponed so that an old prison-ship officer can be found to confirm his identity. Jaggers says there is no hope of acquittal and blames Pip for letting the money be confiscated. Herbert suggests that Pip become a clerk with Clarriker, but Pip has thoughts in another direction. Herbert leaves for the East where Clara will join him once Bill Barley has died. He is glad that Clara, unlike his mother, has no cause for snobbery. Wemmick, regretting the loss of Magwitch's 'portable property', explains that he thought Compeyson was absent when he chose the day for the escape. It must have been Compeyson's plan to misinform Wemmick through his friends in Newgate. Compeyson probably expected a reward for Magwitch's capture. Pip attends Wemmick's wedding to Miss Skiffins and promises not to mention it to Jaggers.

NOTES AND GLOSSARY
Wemmick's wedding is a comic interlude between the drama of the previous chapter and the solemnity of the next. The gap between Wemmick's home life and his profession is as large as ever. Note the emphasis on marriage (Wemmick and Miss Skiffins, Herbert and Clara). We wonder if Pip will find a wife.

the red book: giving the titles and addresses of the aristocracy
Hymen: classical goddess of marriage
Provided by contract: paid in advance

Chapter 56

The condition of Magwitch grows worse, but he does not complain. The trial is short, and, on the last day of Sessions, Magwitch is among thirty-two people condemned to death. He behaves with dignity, reminding the Judge that he has already been sentenced by the Almighty. Pip makes formal petitions for mercy without result and visits Magwitch daily in the prison hospital. On the tenth day Magwitch is very weak. He thanks Pip for his faithfulness. Pip at last tells him that his lost daughter is alive, that she is beautiful, and that he loves her. Magwitch kisses Pip's hand and dies peacefully.

NOTES AND GLOSSARY
In a scene where we could expect Dickens to reflect on the brutality of British law, we get a more universal comment: all human justice is imperfect compared to the judgment of God who sees all men with

'absolute equality'. The religious perspective is also present in the last words of the chapter. In Christ's parable (Luke, XVIII: 10–14) the proud Pharisee thanks God that he is virtuous, while the humble publican asks for mercy on his sins. We remember that for most of the novel Pip has behaved like the Pharisee.

nosegays: bunches of flowers to disguise the unpleasant smell
gewgaws: trivial decorations
Home Secretary: minister for internal affairs in Britain; he has the power to commute a death-sentence

Chapter 57

Pip is nearly arrested for debt and falls dangerously ill. When he recovers he finds Joe who has been sent by Biddy to look after him. He recognises in Joe 'this gentle Christian man'. Joe proudly sends a letter to Biddy who has taught him how to write. He tells Pip that Miss Havisham has died, leaving four thousand pounds to Matthew Pocket and derisive legacies to her fawning relatives. Orlick has been imprisoned for robbing Pumblechook. Joe has heard about Pip's experience with Magwitch but avoids the topic. Instead, he explains why he failed to protect Pip from Mrs Joe. It seems that his attempts to protect Pip only made Mrs Joe more vicious with the boy. Pip improves and Joe leaves secretly after paying Pip's debts. Pip decides to follow him to ask forgiveness. He will also apologise to Biddy, propose marriage, and let her decide whether he should follow Herbert to the East or remain at the forge.

NOTES AND GLOSSARY
Joe is a 'gentle Christian man'. For a discussion of this crucial phrase consult the Commentary, Part 3 (p.63). Notice how Dickens distributes rewards and punishments to the minor characters. Joe's explanations about Mrs Joe may seem unnecessary: in fact, they provide a good example of his gentle tact. Instead of hearing Pip apologise, he prefers to apologise himself.

coddleshell: Joe's version of 'codicil', a legal addition to a will
flowering annuals: plants that have a complete life-cycle in one year

Chapter 58

Pip finds that Satis House is to be pulled down and the furniture sold. At the Blue Boar he finds Pumblechook who sees Pip's misfortunes as a punishment for ingratitude towards his 'earliest benefactor'. Pip walks to the village and is surprised to find Biddy's school closed and no sign of work at the forge. He discovers that he has arrived on the wedding day of Joe and Biddy. Recovering from his first shock, he feels glad that he told Joe nothing about his own hopes of marrying Biddy. He congratulates them, asks and receives forgiveness, and takes a brief emotional farewell. He joins Herbert and Clara in the East as a clerk for Clarriker, pays his debts, and rises to become third in the firm. Clarriker eventually tells Herbert the secret of his partnership. The firm does very well thanks to Herbert's efficiency and Pip's hard work.

NOTES AND GLOSSARY
The landscape, once bleak and threatening, now seems calm and fruitful, reflecting Pip's new moral outlook. Marriage to Biddy is a fitting reward for Joe: it also leaves the way open for Pip's final union with Estella. Note that Pip's eventual prosperity comes from a number of sources: first, Pip's own generosity in arranging a partnership for Herbert; second, Magwitch's fortune which provided the first five hundred pounds; third, Miss Havisham who added the remaining nine hundred. But, ultimately, Pip's success is the result not of mysterious 'great expectations', but of his own hard work.

Chapter 59

Returning to the forge after eleven years abroad, Pip finds Joe and Biddy with their little son (also called Pip). Pip and the boy revisit the churchyard together. Biddy hopes that Pip will marry and mentions Estella, but Pip replies that he no longer has that dream. Nevertheless, he intends to visit Satis House for Estella's sake. He knows that Drummle, who treated her brutally, was killed by a horse two years before. Nothing is left of Satis House except the wall of the old garden. In the evening mist he sees Estella who has come to take a last farewell of the land which is to be sold for building. Her beauty is no longer fresh, but still majestic. She says that suffering has taught her to understand Pip's feelings and she hopes they 'will continue friends apart'. But Pip takes her hand, and, as the rising moon scatters the mist, sees 'no shadow of another parting from her'.

NOTES AND GLOSSARY
The final chapter is pervaded by memories of the past as Pip revisits the scenes of his childhood. At first, the atmosphere is sober and resigned: the happiness of Joe and Biddy is something Pip can only appreciate from the outside. Finally, however, Dickens provides a happy ending for him. Dickens originally wrote a less optimistic conclusion (see A note on the text, Part 1, and also Part 3, Commentary).

Part 3

Commentary

The plot

It is generally agreed that *Great Expectations* has a coherent and concentrated plot. Dickens's other novels usually include subplots which are only tenuously linked to the main theme. In *Great Expectations* all the events and characters are bound together in the same plot.

The plot is divided into three distinct sections of roughly equal length. The first section deals with Pip's childhood in Kent, the second with his life in London, and the third with his attempt to save Magwitch. The three sections correspond broadly to three stages in the moral education of Pip. In the first section we see his dissatisfaction with his status, his essential loneliness, and his first contacts both with a socially superior world (Satis House) and with the underworld of criminality (Magwitch). In the second section he deliberately cuts himself off from his humble origins (Joe and Biddy) and attaches excessive importance to class distinctions, while still not escaping from the taint of the underworld (Jaggers's office, Newgate Prison). In the third section social status and the underworld are brought together through the complex circumstances that link Magwitch not only with Pip, but also with Miss Havisham and Estella. These circumstances lead Pip to a new moral awareness in which he can help Magwitch, forgive Miss Havisham, and be forgiven by Joe.

As always in Dickens, the plot relies heavily on coincidence. It is an incredible coincidence that Magwitch should meet the very boy who will later be invited to Satis House and that Magwitch himself should be linked to Miss Havisham through Compeyson and that Estella should be Magwitch's daughter. Again, it is a coincidence that Jaggers should be the lawyer for both Magwitch and Miss Havisham. These coincidences, however, are not used simply for the sake of sensation or as an arbitrary way of linking isolated subplots to the main story. The plot of *Great Expectations* is a tightly-woven unit and the coincidences all serve to stress the idea that society must be considered as an organic whole and not as a series of isolated units. At first sight, it would seem that the upper class world of Satis House, the criminal underworld of Magwitch, and the village society of Pip and Joe have nothing to do with each other. When Pip tells a fantastic tale about his first visit to

Satis House, his hearers believe him without doubt precisely because they consider Satis House as another world. But Dickens wants to go beyond appearances to show that no section of society really exists in isolation. To do this he creates a series of coincidences which dramatise the links between the classes. Pip, as the hero, becomes the centre in which all classes meet since he is a village boy who becomes a gentleman with the help of a criminal. The coincidences are basically incredible, but they serve to demonstrate a very credible view of society. It is, above all, the coherence of the plot that makes it acceptable even though it is so improbable. When we say that a plot is coherent, we mean that there is some kind of order, some kind of consequence in its development. This is surely the case with *Great Expectations*. The major coincidence, the linking of Magwitch and Miss Havisham in the person of Pip, is established in the first few chapters of the book. All the later coincidences only draw the links more tightly. The whole plot of the novel grows out of the first two episodes (Pip's encounters with Magwitch and Miss Havisham) and develops a significant relation between them.

We noticed in the Introduction that Dickens's plots often follow a fairy-tale pattern where the humble hero turns out to be a prince in disguise. *Great Expectations* uses this pattern only to turn it upside down. Pip dreams of becoming a gentleman, and, when Jaggers announces his 'great expectations', it seems that the fairy tale has become true with Miss Havisham as a fairy godmother, Estella as a princess, and Pip as a male Cinderella. But Pip, as a gentleman, does not move into a glittering world of pleasure where he lives 'happily ever after': instead, he finds himself in the corrupt and sordid world of London. The beautiful princess turns out to be a hard-hearted flirt, and the fairy godmother is much more like a witch. Part of Pip's education involves learning that life is not like a fairy tale, though it may occasionally be like the Eastern story of the doomed sultan (Chapter 38). When Pip learns this lesson, he can start to rebuild his life on a more solid basis.

If the plot of *Great Expectations* is, in many ways, an inverted fairy tale, it is also very obviously a mystery story. At the end of the first part we know that Pip has a mysterious benefactor, but we do not know who it is. Pip assumes that it is Miss Havisham and Dickens gives the reader a great deal of circumstantial evidence (Jaggers is her lawyer, Matthew Pocket is her cousin) to support this view. But he has also planted a number of clues which point in another direction. There is the strange man with the file (Chapter 10), there is Miss Havisham's solemn assertion that Pip can expect nothing more from her (Chapter 13), and there is the determined reticence of Jaggers. Like any good writer of mystery stories, Dickens keeps the reader guessing, giving him some valid clues, but surrounding them with a mass of misleading circumstantial evidence.

Finally, we should notice that the mystery Pip has to solve is the mystery of his own fortune which is ultimately the secret of his real identity. Until Pip knows the source of his wealth, he cannot know himself. *Great Expectations*, like so many novels told in the first person singular, can be read as the narrator's quest for his true identity. In Pip's case this means learning to see identity in moral rather than social terms.

Themes

What is a gentleman?

The major theme of *Great Expectations* can be stated in the form of a simple question: what is a gentleman? The word 'gentleman' is, of course, ambiguous. It may be used to indicate various kinds of high social status, involving wealth, education, and sophisticated manners, or it may serve to define high moral qualities. If we say 'he has the income of a gentleman', we are using a social definition of the word: if we say 'gentlemen don't tell lies', we are thinking in moral terms. But very often, in everyday speech, we tend to confuse the moral and social definitions of 'gentleman', and, in doing so, we run the risk of automatically associating high social status with moral superiority. *Great Expectations* teaches us to distinguish between social prestige and moral worth. Pip's social rise is accompanied by a moral decline, and it is only when his 'great expectations' collapse that he is able to become a gentleman in the moral sense.

The word 'gentleman' recurs in the novel. It is what critics sometimes call a *leitmotif* (originally a musical term borrowed from German to indicate a theme that is repeated with special significance). Almost every time the word is used we should look at the context and at the speaker to see how it is defined. In Chapter 17 Pip confesses to Biddy that he wants to be a gentleman for Estella's sake. At this stage it is clear that being a gentleman means, for Pip, a romantic escape from humble routine. It is associated with the broad prospect and with ships sailing off to adventure. Pip's uncontrolled gestures (pulling up the grass, tearing his hair) show how far he is from any real idea of gentlemanly behaviour. In Chapter 18 the idea of being a gentleman takes a very concrete and unromantic shape. For Jaggers, the practical lawyer, gentility means wealth, and Pip will be a gentleman simply because he can now afford it. Pip, however, immediately falls into the snobbish habit of associating social status with moral superiority. He speaks of raising Joe to 'a higher sphere' and dreams of his future condescending generosity towards the villagers (Chapter 19). He obviously assumes that becoming rich has made him a better man and that he deserves to be admired for it. Pumblechook and Biddy offer contrasting perspectives on Pip's new status. Pumblechook increases Pip's conceit by repeating 'well deserved': Biddy tries unsuccessfully to correct it with the reminder that an honest worker like Joe may also take a justifiable pride in his position.

Pip's arrival in London raises some doubt about the real benefits of gentility. There is an irony, an incongruity between expectation and event, in the fact that Pip's new wealth leads him away from the broad prospect of sea and sky into the narrow streets of the city, and from the comforting warmth of the forge to the squalor of Barnard's Inn. We are also surprised to see that Pip's money, the source of his gentility, comes to him through the disreputable and tainted agency of Jaggers's office. Money, it seems, is not quite a synonym for gentility. Dickens brings the point home to us (if not to Pip) by introducing Herbert Pocket who has very little money, but is unquestionably a gentleman. He is, of course, a gentleman in the social sense because he has received an upper-class education; but already the moral aspect is involved. Herbert teaches Pip elegant table manners, but he reminds us that manners are meaningless unless they derive from sound moral principles. Miss Havisham's lover (Compeyson) had possessed a superficial elegance, and yet, as Herbert's father said, 'no man who was not a true gentleman at heart, ever was, since the world began, a true gentleman in manner'. Pip is still a long way from learning this lesson, but the reader readily applies it to him.

Pip, of course, is not totally insensitive or hopelessly corrupt. If he were, we would not be so distressed at seeing him behave as he does. Although he behaves badly during Joe's visit to London, he still has the decency to recognise the blacksmith's 'simple dignity' and to be seized with remorse. The remorse, unfortunately, is late and ineffectual, and this is typical of the way Pip behaves in the central section of the novel. We see that he has basically good instincts which are constantly frustrated by the power of social pretensions. In fact, Pip's false idea of gentility has become a prison which forces him into futile social gestures such as keeping a useless servant or joining the Finches Club. It is a positive sign that Pip is never self-satisfied for very long. He knows that his way of life is unsatisfactory, although he still does not acknowledge the moral roots of his frustration.

Estella plays a complex and crucial role in Pip's aspirations towards gentility. Pip says that he wants to be a gentleman for her sake (Chapter 17) and it soon becomes clear that, in his desire for her, romantic dreaming and social pretension are inextricably mingled. In Chapter 29 Pip begins by seeing himself as the 'young Knight of romance' who will do 'shining deeds' and 'marry the Princess', but ends by neglecting Joe on the grounds that Estella would despise him. It is hard to separate the romantic dreamer from the snob, and yet, in Chapter 44, we surely recognise that Pip's love has an intense and unselfish quality that raises it above the level of personal ambition.

Both the romantic dream and the social pretension are destroyed by the return of Magwitch (Chapter 39). Magwitch repeats the word 'gentleman' with obsessive determination, and everything he says undermines Pip's false ideas of gentility. Pip's wealth, far from raising him to a higher sphere, associates him with a despised convict. The independence that wealth is supposed to bring turns out to be a sham when Magwitch boasts that he now owns a gentleman. Finally, wealth is no longer seen as a way towards romantic love, but rather as a crude instrument of power, Magwitch's way of taking revenge on the judge and the colonist.

Yet the catastrophe is also a liberation. Released from the prison of false gentility, Pip's better instincts are now free to operate. The change is obvious in two ways. First, Pip starts to think about other people rather than himself. In his interview with Miss Havisham, his first thoughts are for Herbert; when he hears that Estella is to marry Drummle, he is more concerned for her future than for his own. Second, in his efforts to save Magwitch, Pip becomes at last a man of action, whereas previously he has been almost entirely passive.

The basic test of Pip's moral revival lies, of course, in his relations with Magwitch and Joe. Magwitch comes first because it is he, not Joe, who needs Pip's help. It is in serving Magwitch that Pip will become worthy of Joe's friendship and forgiveness. We remember that it was Joe who first recognised in Magwitch a 'poor miserable fellow-creatur''. Pip's service to Magwitch is, significantly, a moral one. Magwitch fails to escape, but he finds in Pip the affection that he has always lacked and can thus meet his death with tranquil dignity. Pip, in his turn, learns from Magwitch that genuine love and self-sacrifice can exist even in an outcast from society. In the great trial scene (Chapter 56) he sees a 'broad shaft of light' linking the Judge to the prisoner and is reminded how 'both were passing, with absolute equality, to the greater Judgment'. In the light of an absolute moral standard, social distinctions become irrelevant.

There remains Pip's recognition of Joe as 'this gentle Christian man' (Chapter 57). The phrase is beautifully exact because it asserts the primacy of moral gentility while admitting the inevitability of social distinctions. Joe cannot simply be called a 'gentleman' because the word has social overtones and we know that Joe will never be a gentleman in the accepted social sense. By breaking up the noun and inserting the adjective 'Christian', Dickens forces us to distinguish between the social and the moral. Being a 'gentleman' is less important than being a 'gentle man'.

The sense of the ending

At the end of the novel Pip returns to England as a moderately wealthy man and marries Estella. This, at first reading, may seem like a dangerous concession to the Victorian taste for happy endings. Is it not inconsistent that Dickens, after exposing the viciousness of snobbery, should give his hero all that a snob desires? Pip, indeed, gets everything: money, respectability, a beautiful wife, even the moral satisfaction of being loved by the lower classes as represented by Joe and Biddy. Why does Dickens begin by condemning Pip's social ambitions and end by satisfying them?

Our answer might start with another question: what would be the alternative? Could Dickens have sent the reformed Pip back to a humble life at the forge? Not really. Pip may understand the difference between moral worth and social status, but he has, nonetheless, been educated as a gentleman. Social distinctions may have no moral basis, and, in an ideal world, they might not exist. But Pip must live in the real world and his place inevitably is with the upper classes. A return to the forge would be highly improbable and morally far too simple.

The Introduction to these Notes (p.11) quoted George Orwell who said that 'Dickens's criticism of society is almost exclusively moral'. In *Great Expectations* there is little evidence that Dickens wants to attack the class system as such. What he attacks is the idea that social status reflects some intrinsic superiority. Social ambition is not wrong in itself: it becomes wrong when it involves condescension, cruelty, or indifference towards the poor and blind admiration of the rich. When Pip finally becomes a gentleman, he does so without false ideas about what gentility means. Moreover, Pip's gentility is no longer a gift from above: it is achieved largely by eleven years' hard work. In this, no doubt, Dickens reflects the views of his audience who believed in 'self-help' and admired men who rose socially as the result of their own honest efforts. Yet even here Dickens refuses to simplify. Pip prospers because he collaborates with Herbert, and the money for Herbert's partnership comes originally from Magwitch. Pip does not inherit a fortune from his convict, but he does get what the Victorians would have called 'a start in life'. It is no more and no less than he deserves.

Pip's final reunion with Estella presents a rather different problem. The question is not whether Pip deserves to marry Estella, but whether Estella could ever make a suitable wife for a man who has rebuilt his life on a new moral basis. Is it likely that man who has rejected snobbery would marry the heartless beauty who was a partial cause of that snobbery? Many readers will prefer the original ending in which Pip and Estella remained apart. Yet even in the original ending we are told that suffering has given Estella a new heart. If this is the case, why should she be prevented from expiating her fault and contributing to Pip's happiness? It may be objected that Estella's reformation is unconvincing since it is presented in a few sentences, whereas Pip's development is demonstrated in detail. The question remains open to debate. In the long run, our answer will depend on how far we share Dickens's confidence in the human capacity for moral renewal.

Isolation

The moral gentleman, as we have seen, is one whose human sympathies are not limited by considerations of social class. The greatest crime, against society and against oneself, is the denial of human fellowship. This crime does not always derive from social causes, but it usually has social consequences.

The most obvious case of deliberate isolation from human fellowship is Miss Havisham. Because her love was once betrayed she attempts to retreat from all human sympathy. Her wealth, which could have been a means of doing good, becomes a source of social evil, encouraging the hypocrisy of fawning relatives, dehumanising Estella, and raising false hopes in Pip. Yet her greatest crime is against herself in hardening the heart that was once capable of a generous though unwise affection. And her greatest punishment is to understand too late that she still needs love. She educates Estella to be heartless, and forgets that Estella will be heartless towards her.

Estella herself is another example of willed isolation, although not quite so guilty as Miss Havisham since she is the victim of her education. Nevertheless, for most of the novel, she seems to take an active pleasure in her role as heartless avenger. Once again, denial of human fellowship has social consequences since she is partly responsible for Pip's snobbery and the suffering it causes to Joe and Biddy. Like Miss Havisham, she is caught in her own trap when she enters a loveless marriage with Drummle. However heartless one tries to be, there is always someone still more heartless. So it is that Estella punishes Miss Havisham, and Drummle punishes Estella. Drummle himself is such an inhuman beast that he can only be punished by the horse that kills him.

Jaggers provides a rather different case of isolation, what might be called isolation within the system. Unlike Miss Havisham or Magwitch, he has no motive for revenge against a society that makes him prosperous and powerful: unlike Estella, he takes no particular pleasure in making others suffer. But his power and prosperity are based on the fact that he deliberately rejects real human involvement and substitutes the mechanical processes of the law. The legal system is his way of avoiding personal responsibility for the fate of his fellow creatures. He is characterised by the gesture of washing his hands. And yet, as we learn in Chapter 51, there was an occasion when he stepped out of his role as agent of the system in order to save a poor child (Estella). For a brief moment the legal mask is dropped: the effect is only to make us realise more poignantly the extent to which Jaggers has let his profession imprison his better instincts.

If Jaggers is isolated *within* the system, Magwitch is isolated *by* the system. His first memory (Chapter 42) is of being cold, hungry, and abandoned, and society has been able to offer him nothing but preaching and prison. His reaction, like that of Miss Havisham (but how much more justified!) is to create an agent for his revenge. As Miss Havisham uses Estella, so Magwitch uses Pip. There, however, the resemblance stops. Magwitch has not willed his own isolation. Though socially an outcast, he is not devoid of human sympathy, and his patronage of Pip is motivated by gratitude as well as revenge. When he gets to know Pip as an individual and not merely as 'my gentleman', the revenge motive gradually disappears. Magwitch, who of all characters had the best reasons for disbelieving in human fellowship, becomes at last one of those who affirm it most strongly.

A Victorian concern

A thematic approach to *Great Expectations* might start out from a number of contrasts or confrontations: the natural or instinctive sense of justice versus the legal system, the outcast versus society, willed isolation versus human commitment, inherited fortune versus personal achievement. It is, however no accident that the major theme which includes and illuminates all the others is the idea of a gentleman.

The Victorian Age was particularly concerned with defining a gentleman. In the old agricultural society gentility had been based largely upon the inherited possession of land. Most gentlemen were gentlemen by birth, and class distinctions were relatively clear and stable. The Industrial Revolution led to an increase in social mobility: people rose more easily from one class to another, and social distinctions became fluid and complex. As a result, many Victorian thinkers worked towards a new definition of the gentleman in which morality and education would become at least as important as wealth or inheritance. Cardinal Newman (1801–90), Matthew Arnold (1822–88), and John Ruskin (1819–1900) all discussed this problem. Tennyson's famous poem, *Idylls of the King* (begun in 1859) was thought to portray the ideal gentleman in the person of Arthur, the legendary British king. In the long run, the Victorians did not reject the social definition of a gentleman, but they added to it the idea of gentility as a moral and intellectual ideal to which all men could aspire.

Great Expectations clearly belongs to the mid-Victorian period when the idea of a gentleman was such a vital topic for discussion. As one might expect, given the limits of his own education, Dickens pays less attention than other Victorians to the intellectual aspect of gentility. We are told that Pip studied hard with Matthew Pocket, but we know practically nothing about what he learned. Many Victorian thinkers tended to see intellectual training as the link between the social and the moral: in *Great Expectations* Pip's formal education has little to do with the growth of moral awareness, though it does, inevitably, make him a gentleman in the social sense.

In conclusion, we may say that *Great Expectations*, although it is set in a pre-Victorian period (1810–30), deals with a basically Victorian problem. According to Humphry House, Dickens shares 'Magwitch's belief that money and education can make a "gentleman" '. This is, perhaps, too simple. Throughout the novel Dickens insists on the limits of mere social gentility. Like many other great Victorians, he relies on a new moral awareness to soften and humanise class distinctions. Pip, in fact, becomes the new gentleman whose social status does not prevent him from possessing a broad human sympathy which transcends social barriers. With this in mind, we can still agree with House when he says that *Great Expectations* is the 'expression of a time when the whole class-drift was upward and there was no reason to suppose that it would ever stop being so'.*

*Humphry House, *The Dickens World*, Oxford University Press, London, 1961, p.155

Style

The two most obvious merits of Dickens's style are fluency and variety. Fluency was, of course, absolutely necessary for a novelist who wrote in monthly or weekly instalments. Nevertheless, few English writers have had such an unforced mastery over the language. We seldom get the impression that Dickens has to struggle with words to make them express his meaning. Indeed, the style of Dickens often seems so easy and natural that we may fail to notice its real precision and subtlety.

It is difficult to illustrate Dickens's style without lengthy quotation. One thing that strikes us immediately is the keen eye for visual detail. Just think of the way Dickens presents a building or a room. Not content with a general description of the setting, he seizes on the significant details that make us see for ourselves: the fire that seems reluctant to burn in Miss Havisham's room, Jaggers's chair of 'deadly black horse-hair, with rows of brass nails round it, like a coffin', the 'crippled flower-pot, cracked glass' in the windows of Barnard's Inn. Or again, to take a very small example of Dickens's precision, notice the adjectives used to describe the money in Chapter 10: 'two fat sweltering one-pound notes'. The 'sweltering' reminds us of the many hot hands that have held the money; 'fat' gives a sense of greasiness and also of complacent opulence.

One characteristic of Dickens's prose that should not be missed is his habit of mechanising individuals and animating objects, or, to put it more simply, making people like things and things like people. Thus Wemmick has 'a post-office of a mouth' (Chapter 21), while the houses 'twisted themselves to peep down at me' (Chapter 20). This device forces us to visualise. Dorothy Van Ghent suggests that it also reflects an industrial society where men become dehumanised and objects assume a terrifying power.* An extreme example of this threatening life of objects is provided by the room at the Hummums Hotel where Pip passes such a wretched night (Chapter 45).

The sensitivity of Dickens to varieties of spoken English hardly needs demonstration. It should be enough to say that no two characters in *Great Expectations* speak in the same way. There is the bullying Jaggers who starts half his sentences with 'Now' or 'Very well' as if he wanted to cut off further discussion; there is Magwitch with his distorted verbs (correcting them would be an excellent exercise!); there is Joe's hopelessly confused syntax, Herbert's easy conversation, Biddy's plain speaking, Miss Havisham's melodramatic rhetoric. Even where the idiom seems highly improbable, as it does in Joe's case, it still seems to fit the

*Dorothy Van Ghent, *The English Novel: Form and Function*, Holt, Rinehart and Winston, New York, 1953, pp.128–31.

character so well that we cannot think of him without it. Lower-class speech habits, however, do not always render a character comic or inexpressive. Both Joe and Magwitch can rise to an impressive eloquence (Joe in Chapter 27, 'Life is made of ever so many partings': Magwitch in Chapter 54, 'We'd be puzzled to be more quiet'). This powerful use of lower-class idiom is not merely a sign of Dickens's variety: it is evidence of a genuinely democratic approach to language. Eloquence is not reserved for the upper classes.

The first-person narrative is superbly flexible and moves easily from solemn pathos to comic observation, and from meditation to rapid action. The first five chapters, for example, offer a brilliant mixture of atmospheric suggestion (the marsh landscape), psychological insight (Pip's self-awareness and guilt), broad comedy (Pumblechook drinking the tar-water), and dramatic activity (the capture of the convicts). Another masterpiece of narrative is Chapter 54. The pace is carefully varied, but it never loses tension. The crowded bustling river gives way to the ominous calm of the estuary; this is followed by an expectant pause at the inn, and we end with a burst of violence as Magwitch and Compeyson go down together.

The qualities so far described could be found in most of Dickens's novels. *Great Expectations*, however, has a style of its own. Graham Greene, a fine contemporary novelist, has spoken of 'the tone of Dickens's secret prose, that sense of a mind speaking to itself with no one there to listen, as we find it in *Great Expectations*'.* This 'secret prose' comes from the novelist's subtle way of reminding us that the narrator of the story is no longer an immature youth but an experienced man who looks back on his earlier life and tries to see its meaning. Pip's youthful experiences may be recreated with vivid immediacy, but we are also made aware of the older man who has learned what these experiences were worth. Sometimes we even feel that the novel is not so much a story told by Pip to the reader, but a private dialogue between the older Pip (the narrator) and the younger Pip (the protagonist). The attentive reader will soon recognise the moments when the mature narrator intervenes with judgment or comment. The comment, however, need not be explicit. It can be implied in the way a scene is presented. In Chapter 17 where Pip behaves so badly towards Biddy, the whole tone and quality of observation suggests the mature Pip taking an ironic and embarrassed look at his former self. Another notable example is the opening of Chapter 29 where Pip's infatuation with Estella is first presented in exaggerated romantic terms and then subjected to a cool

*Graham Greene, 'The Young Dickens' in *The Lost Childhood and Other Essays*, Penguin Books, Harmondsworth, 1962, p.57.

and lucid analysis. In the third and final section of the novel, the gap between Pip the protagonist and Pip the narrator is closed. The snobbish dreamer has become the humane clear-sighted man who can recount his own life with honesty and objectivity. This is stylistic achievement of a rare quality. It is the answer to some of Dickens's early critics who thought that because he was popular, he must be simple and unsophisticated.

Humour

Great Expectations is not a comic novel. The dominant tone is that of the narrator, sober, saddened, and ironic. And yet the novel contains some of Dickens's most successful humour. That Dickens had a comic vein in mind from the start is clear from his letter to Forster:

> You will not have to complain of the want of humour as in the *Tale of Two Cities*. I have made the opening, I hope, in its general effect exceedingly droll. I have put a child and a good-natured foolish man in relations that seem to me very funny. Of course I have got in the pivot on which the story will turn too—and which indeed, as you remember, was the grotesque tragi-comic conception that first encouraged me.*

Obviously, as the novel proceeded, this comic intention was modified, especially in the relations between Pip and Joe. But the revealing phrase is 'tragi-comic conception'. It warns us that in *Great Expectations* the comic and serious elements will be closely linked. It is, in fact, a great achievement that the comedy serves to intensify and enhance the serious concerns of the novel rather than detracting attention from them.

We can demonstrate this by looking at some of the comic characters. They are mostly created in Dickens's usual fashion, with peculiarities of appearance and speech that resemble caricature. But they are also significantly linked to the main theme of the book. Wopsle, Mrs Matthew Pocket, and, to some extent, Wemmick parody respectively the romantic, snobbish, and financial aspects of Pip's 'great expectations'. Wopsle, like Pip, feels himself excluded from fame and fortune. He cannot become a clergyman because the Church of England has not been 'thrown open' to the lower classes. Instead, he nourishes the romantic dream of 'reviving the Drama' just as Pip sees himself as 'the young Knight of romance'. Pip, in fact, subconsciously links his own

*Letter to John Forster, in *Charles Dickens: A Critical Anthology*, Ed. Stephen Wall, Penguin Books, Harmondsworth, 1970, pp.155–6.

expectations to those of Wopsle when, in a nightmare, he has to 'play
Hamlet to Miss Havisham's Ghost' (Chapter 31).

Mrs Matthew Pocket is related to the snobbish side of Pip. She
regards herself as a superior being simply because she is the daughter
of a knight: in the same way Pip expects to be admired simply because
he is now a gentleman. Moreover, just as Mrs Pocket's assumed social
status makes her 'perfectly helpless and useless' as a wife and mother
(Chapter 23), so Pip's gentility puts him in a position which is 'not
beneficial to anybody' (Chapter 34).

Wemmick, of course, is more complex since he has positive qualities
that Wopsle and Mrs Matthew Pocket lack. Nonetheless, in his insist-
ence on the need for 'portable property' he parodies the financial aspect
of Pip's expectations. The theme of inheritance (which also applies to
the self-seeking relatives who fawn on Miss Havisham) is rendered
concrete and visual when we see Wemmick dressed in the relics he has
been given by condemned criminals. Wemmick, at least, has the honesty
to acknowledge his motives. It is ironic that Pip's expectations, like
Wemmick's 'portable property', should be inherited from a criminal.

None of these characters is subjected to severe moral condemnation.
Wopsle and Mrs Pocket are comically pathetic: Wemmick is comically
eccentric. Pumblechook, however, is singled out for the most biting
humour, perhaps because hypocrisy is the vice that Dickens most
detests. Other characters may deceive themselves; Pumblechook tries
to deceive the whole world, as we can see from the newspaper article
that presents him as the founder of Pip's fortunes and the friend of his
youth (Chapter 28). Pumblechook, perhaps, is the one comic character
in the novel who tends to get out of control. In Chapter 13 the sequence
of epithets ('detested seedsman', 'fearful impostor', 'abject hypocrite',
etc.) is a joke that goes on too long: so is the repetition of 'May I?' in
Chapter 19. Nevertheless, Pumblechook is a character the reader would
not want to miss. Like the comic characters of Dickens's earlier novels,
he is not a credible human being, but a wonderful caricature, larger
than life, inflated by his creator's exuberance. The vigour and vividness
of Pumblechook suggest how much Dickens loved to invent characters
he could hate.

The humour of Dickens is not limited to the invention of characters.
Great Expectations abounds in sheer verbal humour. We can illustrate
this with a few examples from Chapter 4. Mrs Joe speaks of 'formal
cramming and busting' and the joke lies in the contrast between the
polite adjective and the vulgar nouns: she goes to church 'vicariously'
with a pun on 'vicar', a priest in the Church of England. Joe is dressed
in 'penitentials' suggesting both religious penitence and also the peni-

tentiary (prison). At the forge Pip and Joe find 'Mrs Joe dressed, and the dinner dressing', an unusual association between cooking and clothes. The point of the conversation gets stuck into Pip who is like 'an unfortunate little bull in a Spanish arena'. Pip is brought up 'by hand', and the phrase suggests both rough primitive methods of production and also the literal physical violence he endures.

Humour of this kind is, of course, more subtle than the humour that makes Pumblechook, and certainly requires closer attention on the reader's part. It reminds us that the comic gift of Dickens is not limited to glorious caricatures. Once again we are impressed by the varied humour that can invent the hilarious physical comedy of Pumblechook drinking the tar-water, and, in the same chapter, show a sophisticated and witty use of language.

Symbolism

Many critics have discussed the symbolism of Dickens's novels. They usually show that the specific characters and events represent permanent forces and patterns in human life. Seen in this light, Jaggers becomes 'the representative not only of civil law but of universal Law'; Joe and Orlick, because they are both uneducated men, embody the extremes of love and hate possible in primitive human nature; Pip and Magwitch work out the eternal pattern of redemption from sin through love and self-sacrifice.*

All this, however, means only that *Great Expectations*, like all major literature, deals with issues of permanent significance. It is very easy and not very useful to say that a good man symbolises goodness or a lawyer symbolises law. We should, therefore, look at some more complex examples, especially those where a precise setting or object becomes broadly suggestive because of its function in the story or its relation to a character.

It is, for example, quite conventional to speak of 'the river of time' or 'the flow of life'. But in *Great Expectations* we can see how the Thames functions as a pervasive element, threatening and promising, obscurely controlling the destinies of men. In Chapter 1 the river appears as a threat to Pip, and from it comes Magwitch laden with crime and suffering. By Chapter 17, when Pip is approaching manhood, the river has changed into a promising prospect. In the London section of the book the river is, at first, less obviously present, perhaps because the artificial structures of city life try to ignore or disguise the fluid and unstable elements of existence. With Magwitch's return, however, the

*Dorothy Van Ghent, *The English Novel: Form and Function*, 1953, pp.125–38.

river flows back into the novel. In Chapter 54 Magwitch himself suggests its significance:

> We can no more see to the bottom of the next few hours, than we can see to the bottom of this river what I catches hold of. Nor yet we can't no more hold their tide than I can hold this. And it's run through my fingers and gone, you see!

Both the threat and the promise of the river will be fulfilled. It acts destructively, drowning Compeyson and fatally wounding Magwitch; but it also purifies and liberates, leaving Pip and Magwitch to be redeemed by love. The river does, indeed, work like time, dissolving, transforming, and renewing life.

Another example of symbolism is the wedding cake in Chapter 11. Miss Havisham has tried to arrest her life at the moment of her betrayal, but a life cannot really be arrested: it is always productive of something. If its natural growth is frustrated, it will produce poisonous and perverted growths like the spiders and fungus on the cake. The spiders consume the cake that is their home: in the same way Miss Havisham's passions turn inward and destroy her mind. The spiders also suggest the corruption that Miss Havisham extends to those around her: they are like the parasitic Pockets who will 'feast upon' her when she is dead and laid upon the table where the cake now stands. Miss Havisham, indeed, is so much like the cake that one day she will take its place.

Our two examples show Dickens using two very different kinds of symbol. The cake is an 'illustrative symbol' since its only purpose is to represent a particular mental condition. The river is a 'structural symbol' because it develops, involving a variety of characters and helping to shape the plot. Even without discussing the many other symbols in the novel, we can see why J. Hillis Miller says that 'in *Great Expectations* Dickens's particular view of things is expressed with a concreteness and symbolic intensity he never surpassed'.*

Characterisation

It is often said that Dickens's characters, though vivid and memorable, lack complexity and psychological depth. A famous modern novelist, E.M. Forster, has distinguished between 'flat' and 'round' characters and concluded that most of Dickens's characters are flat.† A flat

---

*J. Hillis Miller, *Charles Dickens: the World of his Novels*, Harvard University Press, Cambridge, Mass., 1958, p.249.
†E.M. Forster, *Aspects of the Novel*, Edward Arnold, London, 1927, pp.93–99.

character usually represents a single idea or quality, revealed by recognisable characteristics such as dress, gesture, or habits of speech. These representative figures can be called types: if their characteristics are deliberately exaggerated, they become caricatures. Jaggers, for example, is a type: Pumblechook is a caricature.

The capacity to imagine types or caricatures is a genuine gift, not a sign that the novelist is simple-minded. By creating a wide variety of types and making them interact the novelist may give a highly complex picture of the forces at work in society. Moreover, we should remember that in social life we do not usually see deeply into the psychology of other people. We recognise them, as we do in Dickens's novels, by their obvious external characteristics. In this sense, we can say that Dickens's method is realistic. He may not always present the reality of complex characters, but he does present the real way in which we see and know people.

As a general rule, it can be said that the treatment of characters as types is suitable for novels whose major concern is social rather than psychological. Some of the greatest novels, however, succeed in combining psychological depth with a broad vision of society. This is certainly the case with *Great Expectations*. We have a broad range of significant social types: the convict Magwitch, the blacksmith Joe, the shopkeeper Pumblechook, the lawyer Jaggers ... But we also have, in Pip, a profound and detailed psychological study. Pip, indeed, unites the social and psychological concerns since his career is shaped both by social forces and by his own innate character.

We can, perhaps, divide the characters of *Great Expectations* into three groups: those who develop, those who are gradually revealed, and those who are immediately obvious. Pip is the clearest example of a developing character, but we should also think of Magwitch and possibly of Estella. They all show an evolution towards moral awareness. In the second group we have figures like Joe, Biddy, Herbert, and Jaggers. There is no evidence that any of these characters develop, but there is a process of gradual revelation. We know them better at the end than we did at the beginning. Finally, we have the immediately obvious characters such as Orlick, Pumblechook, Wopsle, and the parasitic Pockets. From the very start we know who they are and what they represent. No later events will modify our first impressions. There are, of course, a few characters who are more difficult to place. Miss Havisham and Mrs Joe both repent before they die; but their remorse is too sudden for us to think of them as developing characters. They really belong to the second and third groups.

The information given below is intended to help your memory and is divided into two parts: first, brief sketches of all the major characters; second, essential facts about the minor figures with a list in brackets of the chapters where they appear. Remember that you can find more discussion of the major characters in the preceding parts of this Critical Commentary and also in the notes that follow chapter summaries.

The major characters

Pip

Philip Pirrip, known as Pip, is an orphan. Being deprived of maternal affection, he feels insecure. Notice how he feels threatened (Chapter 1) even before the convict appears. His sister, Mrs Joe, regards him as a burden, and this may explain the excessive sense of guilt we see in his reactions to the convict, to his fight with Herbert, and to the attack on Mrs Joe. His attempt to educate himself and his capacity for inventing a story (Chapter 9) show that he is intelligent and imaginative. These qualities help him to look beyond the narrow world of the forge, but they are combined with a 'morally timid and very sensitive' character as a result of his sister's harshness. He is incapable of replying to Estella's insults and he suffers from hallucinations and nightmares. With this sensitive and insecure temperament, it is unlikely that Pip's ambition would ever have gone beyond the forge, had it not been for outside forces represented by Magwitch and Miss Havisham.

In judging Pip's behaviour as a gentleman, we should remember that his first contact with the upper-class world at Satis House is deliberately designed to humiliate him. Moreover, his 'great expectations' come upon him without preparation and without explanation. Under such circumstances, it is hardly surprising that an immature and insecure youth should lose his moral bearings, especially when so many people are eager to flatter him. The sound morality and practical wisdom of Biddy have little chance of influencing him when society as a whole seems to accept the standards of false gentility. In Pip's new situation, his sense of guilt, originally a handicap, becomes a saving grace. Even though Pip's snobbery usually frustrates his better instincts, his mind is never at ease. His recurring sense of dissatisfaction is the best proof that he still has a moral conscience. His delight in Wemmick's home and his generosity towards Herbert show that he can still appreciate the value of human fellowship. Pip's love for Estella intensifies his snobbery and is directly responsible for his neglect of Joe; but it is, after all, a typically adolescent passion. Pip's romantic immaturity makes his snobbery less obnoxious than it would be in a more experienced man. It is, in any case, quite obvious that the mature Pip who tells the story (Pip the narrator) is no longer a snob: if he were, he could not judge his younger self (Pip the protagonist) with such lucid severity. Since we know from the start that Pip will become a better man, we suspend or soften our moral condemnation. In short, although we are forced to condemn Pip's behaviour, we never lose our sympathy for him. Pip's narrative is, indeed, a confession, and we must admire a man who confesses so honestly.

The return of Magwitch destroys the basis of Pip's snobbery. He is now forced to face reality, and, as he does so, he begins to think more of others and less of himself. The need for action saves him from despair. In trying to save Magwitch, he turns away from the distant dreams that have resulted in frustrating idleness. Instead, he finds himself with an immediate and practical purpose. Magwitch, who partly caused Pip's snobbery by giving him 'great expectations', now becomes the instrument of his redemption. It is in serving Magwitch that Pip earns the right to Joe's forgiveness.

Magwitch

Abel Magwitch first appears as little better than an animal, covered with the slime of the marshes, wolfing his food. Notice, however, the strange click in Magwitch's throat which shows the presence of human emotions that he cannot express. His verbal violence towards Pip and his physical violence towards Compeyson make him obviously dangerous, and yet he remains pathetically vulnerable. At this stage, however, only Joe can recognise him as a 'fellow-creature': it will be a long time before Pip can make the same recognition. When he returns he still has the manners of a convict, but we are moved by his childish delight in Pip's gentlemanly appearance and we admire the energy that has made a fortune in Australia. What we learn of his past life absolves him from any real responsibility in his crimes, justifies his hatred of Compeyson, and accounts for his wish to take revenge on society. Society, in its behaviour towards Magwitch, has effectively denied the morality it preaches. It has condemned him as a hardened criminal while giving him no chance to be anything else. But Magwitch is not merely a passive victim: he has shown love for his daughter, loyalty towards Molly, and gratitude to Pip. As affection for Pip replaces the revenge motive and his violent instincts are softened, we see a growth in his moral stature. This is reflected by simple gestures (the reassuring hand on Pip's shoulder in Chapter 54) and by an increased dignity of language. In the trial scene the threatening animal of the marshes has become an eloquent human being who can address the Judge in terms of 'absolute equality'. He has earned Pip's praise of him as 'a much better man than I had been to Joe'.

Joe

Joe Gargery, the 'good-natured foolish man' of Dickens's original idea, emerges finally as the ideal of a 'gentle Christian man'. This is not a development (Joe does not change) but a gradual revelation of character. The first sign of Joe's real nature comes with his recognition of Magwitch as a 'fellow-creature'. Joe's account of his childhood with a brutal father and a suffering mother shows his submissiveness to Mrs Joe as moral sensibility rather than weakness. As for his courage, we notice that he is the only man capable of frightening Jaggers (Chapter 18). Nor is Joe as foolish as we first assume. In warning Pip not to visit Miss Havisham because it might appear that he 'expected something', he shows a truly intelligent tact. It is also significant that he does learn to write when he is taught with love by Biddy and not with condescension by Pip. Even when Pip treats him badly, Joe is never a man to be pitied. Unlike Pip, he has an innate pride and sense of purpose (Chapter 27). It is a pity that Joe's impossible syntax sometimes makes him comic and unconvincing at the wrong moments. It seems as if Dickens did not quite overcome his original comic conception of the character.

Mrs Joe

Pip's sister is a fierce caricature of the aggressive woman, contemptuous of her husband and brutal to the child. The pins and needles at her breast symbolise her lack of maternal instincts. She is hypocritical in presenting herself as a martyr to duty when, in fact, she torments others. She is largely responsible for Pip's chronic sense of insecurity. We almost applaud the attack on her as a deserved punishment. Her final repentance is acceptable only because she has long ceased to be a threat.

Compeyson

Compeyson appears briefly in Chapters 3, 5, 47, and 54, but all our information about him comes from Magwitch and Herbert. He is largely responsible for Magwitch's misfortunes. He knows that Magwitch hid during Molly's trial and uses this knowledge to blackmail him into submission. He then blames Magwitch for his own crimes when they are tried together. Finally, he arranges Magwitch's capture by the police in Chapter 54. As someone who 'set up for a gentleman', he offers a criminal variation on the theme of snobbery. Otherwise, he represents an evil so total and unmotivated that it must remian mysterious.

Pumblechook

Pumblechook is a classic caricature, immediately recognisable by his physical presence (fat, fishy-eyed, sandy-haired), his pompous speech, his gluttony, and his complete insensitivity. Notice the cruel conversation he directs at Pip (Chapter 4) and his disgraceful behaviour at Mrs Joe's funeral (Chapter 35). Apart from accompanying Pip to Satis House, he plays no significant part in the plot, and, on later occasions, Dickens uses him mainly for comic relief. His social pretensions, however, are generally related to the major theme of snobbery.

Miss Havisham

Miss Havisham suffers an emotional shock when she is abandoned by Compeyson. Her reaction is to cut herself off from human fellowship. Her one good action in adopting Estella turns into a crime when she uses the girl as an instrument of revenge. Pip is another victim of Miss Havisham since she allows him to regard her as his benefactor and encourages Estella to torment him. She falls into her own trap when Estella becomes heartless towards her. We should remember, however, that Miss Havisham was once the victim of a generous though unwise passion and that a member of her own family (Arthur) conspired against her. She is a character of extremes: first, ready to give all for love, and then denying love completely. Seen in this light, the suddenness of her repentance seems convincing. Miss Havisham's isolation from normal life is reflected not only in the strange setting of Satis House, but also in her melodramatic way of acting and speaking. It is fitting that she should meet her death in melodramatic circumstances, a victim of her own obsession with the past when her wedding dress catches fire.

Estella

In portraying Pip's relationship with Estella, Dickens gives what may be his only convincing picture of the force of sexual attraction. At a first reading Estella may seem a static character whose final change of heart is unconvincing. Dickens, however, gives us some clues that suggest a development. At the start she is simply the cruel instrument of Miss Havisham's revenge. Later she seems to have some pity for Pip when she warns him that she has no heart. But this is ambiguous. Is it honesty towards someone she does not want to deceive? Or is it a perverse way of attracting Pip by reminding him that she inaccessible? In judging Estella, we should remember that people who really have no heart do not usually announce that they are heartless. One sign of Estella's development is her growing realisation of how Miss Havisham has formed her, culminating in the statement 'I must be taken as I have been made' (Chapter 38). To be so clear about one's unbringing is a step in overcoming it. Estella's marriage to Drummle is the self-destructive act of someone who has taken the wrong road and is too proud to turn back. It may still be argued that Estella's final redemption is unconvincing.

Herbert

Herbert Pocket combines the moral and social qualities of a gentleman. He inherits his father's honesty, warning Pip against Estella just as Matthew Pocket warned Miss Havisham against Compeyson. In his love for Clara he shows that he has none of Pip's snobbery. His tact is evident in his treatment of Joe and Magwitch and in the delicate way he corrects Pip's table manners (Chapter 22). Herbert is, above all, a loyal friend who actively helps Pip in his attempt to save Magwitch. He is, of course, unaware that he has already been rewarded with the five hundred pounds provided for his partnership. At first, Herbert seems unrealistic in his business plans and weak in his imitation of Pip's idle habits. Later we are told that Clarriker's firm owes much of its success to Herbert's 'cheerful industry'. Knowing how to work is one of the marks of a true gentleman. Herbert conforms to his father's ideal. His fine manners show that he is a gentleman at heart (Chapter 22).

Orlick

Orlick has no redeeming features. He seems to come from one of Pip's nightmares. We are told that he likes to frighten the boy with tales of the Devil. His appearances are mysterious, 'as if by mere accident' (Chapter 14). He haunts Pip like a ghost at crucial moments: after the important talk with Biddy (Chapter 17), when Magwitch returns (Chapter 40), and before the decisive interview with Miss Havisham (Chapter 44). In attacking Mrs Joe, he acts obscurely on Pip's behalf, using the weapon (the convict's leg-iron) that Pip has unwittingly provided. It is significant that he attacks Pip directly (Chapter 53) only when Pip is already on the way to redemption. It is as if the growing power of goodness forces evil to show its face. Orlick is eventually arrested for robbing Pumblechook. It may seem strange that this nightmare figure of primitive evil should be reduced to the level of a petty criminal. It may, however, suggest that Pip has nothing more to fear from nightmares.

Biddy

Biddy, a distant relative of Wopsle, is patient, loving, and wise. She also has a practical toughness that makes her more convincing than a sentimental portrait of female perfection. She knows how to defend herself and is not afraid of reproaching Pip when he deserves it (Chapters 17, 19, 35). It is a sign of her realism that she transfers her love to Joe when Pip proves unsuitable. Since she so often speaks for the moral values that Joe embodies, it is fitting that she should marry him. Dickens acknowledges her practical energy and wisdom by making her a teacher in the new school.

Jaggers

Jaggers first seems a caricature of the bullying unscrupulous lawyer, characterised by obvious speech habits ('Now', 'Very well') and gestures (biting and throwing his forefinger). He also seems something of a coward. After humiliating an easy victim in Wopsle, he retreats before Joe (Chapter 18). In his London office he seems to embody the inhumanity of a legal system which puts the letter of law before the spirit of justice. Gradually, however, we see a more complex character. He is clearly fascinated by criminal psychology (delighted to recognise Drummle as 'one of the true sort'), but his constant washing of hands suggests an uneasy conscience. For a time Jaggers seems to hold all the clues to the plot: he is the lawyer for both Miss Havisham and Magwitch, knowing the identity of Pip's benefactor and Estella's mother. But, until Pip tells him, he does not know that Magwitch is Estella's father or that both Magwitch and Miss Havisham are linked to Compeyson. He is, therefore, less powerful than he appears. Jaggers once had his 'poor dreams' and acted nobly in trying to save Estella from a life of misery. Since then he has suppressed his feelings and let himself become identified with the legal system. At the end of Chapter 51 we still see him as the prisoner of his profession. For an example of his professional skill, see his defence of Molly (Chapter 48).

Wemmick

Like Jaggers, Wemmick first appears as a caricature with his post-office mouth and wooden features. Gradually he is revealed as the split personality produced by a dehumanising profession. There is the Little Britain (office) Wemmick and the Walworth (home) Wemmick, both of them with appropriately contrasting sentiments. Notice the different kinds of advice he gives Pip about helping Herbert (Chapters 36, 37). Only once, for Pip's sake, are home and office sentiments allowed to mix (Chapter 51), but this obviously will not happen again. Jaggers will not be told of Wemmick's marriage to Miss Skiffins. Wemmick's treatment of the Aged Parent contrasts with Pip's behaviour to Joe. The warm atmosphere of his eccentric home provides a partial substitute for the forge. Wemmick's obsession with 'portable property' is related to the larger theme of inheritance.

Drummle

Bentley Drummle may be taken as exemplifying the fact that money and social rank do not make a gentleman. Jaggers sees him as a criminal type, but his evil is not mysterious like that of Orlick or Compeyson. He is quite simply a brute. Estella marries him not for wealth, but just because she despises him. He is, however, too brutal to be hurt by a heartless wife and he treats her cruelly. It is fitting that such a brute should be killed by a horse.

The Minor Characters

The Aged Parent. Wemmick's father, deaf but cheerful (25, 37, 45, 55).

Arthur Havisham. Miss Havisham's dissolute half-brother. He inherits less money than Miss Havisham, wastes it, and plots with Compeyson against her. He dies in misery, haunted by the vision of his unhappy half-sister (22, 42).

The Avenger. Pip's name for his superfluous servant, Pepper (27, 30, 34).

Bill Barley. Clara's father, a retired ship's purser, dying of gout, heard cursing in his room (46, 58).

Clara Barley. Herbert's fiancée, lives with her father at Mill Pond Bank where Magwitch shelters before his attempt to escape. At first she resents Pip's bad influence on Herbert, but later grows to like him. After her father's death, she joins Herbert in the East (30, 46, 55, 58).

Mrs Brandley. Estella's hostess at Richmond, a frivolous widow with a theological daughter (38).

Clarriker. A shipping-broker in need of capital. Pip provides five hundred pounds to buy Herbert a partnership in his firm, and Miss Havisham adds the remaining nine hundred. After the collapse of his expectations, Pip becomes a clerk for Clarriker and later a partner in the firm (37, 44, 49, 52, 58).

Mrs Coiler. A toadying neighbour of the Pockets at Hammersmith (23).

Flopson and Millers. Lively independent servants of the Pockets (22, 23, 33).

The Hubbles. Neighbours of Joe Gargery. Pathetically pretentious, they enjoy formal occasions such as Christmas dinner, the feast for Pip's apprenticeship, Mrs Joe's funeral. Mr Hubble is a wheelwright (4, 13, 35).

The Jack. Odd-job man at a riverside inn, dressed in the relics of drowned sailors (54).

Lazarus. Excitable little man who tries unsuccessfully to persuade Jaggers to defend his brother (20).

The Man with the File. A released convict who gives Pip two pounds from Magwitch. Pip overhears him later discussing the episode. He has obviously been rearrested (10, 28).

Mike. A criminal client of Jaggers, always in trouble (20, 51).

Molly. Magwitch's wife, though not legally married, Estella's mother. A jealous woman, she is arrested for murdering a rival and successfully defended by Jaggers who takes her as his housekeeper. She never sees Magwitch or Estella again. One wrist is deeply scarred from her struggle with the victim. Wemmick calls her 'a wild beast tamed' (24,26,42,48,50,51).

Pip Gargery. Son of Joe and Biddy (59).

Matthew Pocket. Herbert's father and Pip's tutor. Well-educated and gentlemanly, he makes a poor living from private teaching and is constantly distracted by his large chaotic family. He warned Miss Havisham against Compeyson, was dismissed from Satis House, and never returned. His honesty is rewarded when Miss Havisham leaves him four thousand pounds (11, 18, 22, 23, 24, 33, 44, 57)

Mrs Matthew Pocket. The daughter of a knight. Her ridiculous snobbery makes her ineffective as wife and mother (22, 23, 30, 33).

Jane Pocket. Herbert's younger sister, more practical than her parents, hopes to get married (22, 23, 30, 33).

Baby Pocket. Always in danger from playing with nutcrackers and needles (22, 23, 33).

Camilla, Sarah, and Georgiana Pocket. Sycophantic relatives who hope to inherit Miss Havisham's wealth. Camilla pretends to suffer in sympathy with Miss Havisham. Sarah stays at Satis House to spy on Miss Havisham when Estella leaves. They conspire against Pip. Miss Havisham torments them by letting them think that she is Pip's benefactor. She leaves them derisive legacies (11, 19, 22, 25, 29, 33, 44, 57).

Raymond. Camilla's husband (11).

The Sergeant. Leads the soldiers in the hunt for Magwitch, drinks cheerfully with Pumblechook (5).

Miss Skiffins. Wemmick's fiancée, later his wife, has mechanical gestures like Wemmick (37, 55).

Startop. A good friend of Pip and Herbert, studies with Matthew Pocket, helps to rescue Pip from Orlick and joins in the attempt to save Magwitch (23, 25, 26, 34, 52, 53, 54).

Trabb. Tailor and funeral director, flatters Pip (19, 35).

Trabb's Boy. An exuberant comedian who twice humiliates Pip, but eventually helps to rescue him from Orlick (19, 30, 53).

Wopsle. Parish clerk in Pip's village. Barred from a career in the Church by his low social status, he dreams of reviving the drama. His *Hamlet* in London is a hilarious failure, and he ends up in pantomime. His impossible ambitions are a parody of Pip's 'great expectations' (4, 5, 6, 7, 10, 13, 15, 18, 27, 31, 47).

Wopsle's Great-Aunt runs the ridiculous evening school in Pip's village (7, 10).

Part 4

Hints for study

Choosing what to study

In studying a novel like *Great Expectations*, there are two golden rules:
(*a*) read with a purpose, and (*b*) be selective.

(*a*) Reading with a purpose means knowing what you are looking for. After your first reading, you will have a general idea of what the novel is about. When you read it a second time, you should be thinking about possible examination topics such as *theme, character, style, setting, humour*. Arrange your notes under these headings, and under each heading indicate the significant chapters with a brief comment. We know, for example, that snobbery is a major theme. Your notes under this heading might begin like this:

Chapter 8   Pip at Satis House, made ashamed of his humble origins. Estella scorns him for his coarse hands and thick boots.

Chapter 13   Pip no longer wants to be a blacksmith.

Chapter 17   Pip dreams of being a gentleman for Estella's sake. He is condescending towards Biddy.

Chapters 18–19   Pip learns of his 'great expectations' and behaves badly to Joe and Biddy. He does not understand what Biddy means when she speaks of Joe's pride.

Chapter 22   Herbert is a true gentleman. He quotes his father who says that 'a true gentleman in manner' must be 'a true gentleman at heart'.

If you carry on with these brief notes to the end of the novel, you will get a good idea of the way Dickens develops the theme of snobbery. Sometimes your note could take the form of a question. On Chapter 17 you might ask 'Is Pip's love for Estella the cause of Pip's snobbery or the result of it?' Many chapters, of course, will have to be noted under more than one heading. Most of the chapters that concern snobbery also concern Pip's character. Chapter 1 is not directly concerned with snobbery, but it would come under the headings of *character, setting*, and, perhaps, *style*. Chapter 17 might require notes under the different headings of *theme, character, setting*, or even *humour*. The important point about having different headings is that it helps you to distinguish between different aspects of the novel and prepares you for specific examination questions.

(*b*) Our second rule was 'be selective'. You cannot hope to remember everything about the novel. If you try, you will only get confused. Even if you can remember a great deal, you will not have time to say or write it all during an examination. Imagine, for example, that you are asked about the character of Pip. Since Pip tells the story, almost every chapter reveals something about him. But in your answer you must concentrate on a few major aspects and select illustrations to make your point. You may say that Pip is sensitive and imaginative, but you cannot mention all the examples that prove this. Select the most obvious ones such as the fantastic story he tells at the forge when he returns from Satis House (Chapter 9) or his vision of Miss Havisham hanging in the brewery (Chapters 8, 49). As an example of Pip's sense of guilt, you might use his reaction to the attack on Mrs Joe (Chapter 16). To demonstrate Pip's snobbery you could discuss Joe's visit to London (Chapter 27). Being selective means avoiding repetition. In an essay on characterisation you would want to show how Dickens conveys character through significant gestures or habits of speech. There are dozens of possible examples, but you should stick to three or four, such as Jaggers throwing his forefinger and washing his hands, Wemmick's post-office mouth, Joe's confused syntax, Magwitch's way of eating. This will leave you time to talk about Pip, Herbert, and Estella who obviously are not characterised in the same way.

Keep your notes short. If you put down too many details, you will fail to remember the basic points. Purposeful and selective notes should include only those points you would use in an examination answer. By the time you take your examination, you should already have decided on the examples you would use to illustrate a given topic.

Quotations

Here again you must be purposeful and selective. The quotations you choose should be short enough for you to remember with reasonable accuracy. Quotations should be used with moderation. An essay without quotations may suggest that you have not read the novel very carefully: an essay crammed with quotations may suggest that you simply learn things by heart without thinking about them. It is not enough to quote. You must show why your quotation is useful.

Frequently you will find that a quotation is a useful way to begin or end an essay. An essay on Pip's character or on the theme of snobbery might begin with Matthew Pocket's statement that 'a true gentleman in manner' must be 'a true gentleman at heart' (Chapter 22) and then show how *Great Expectations* develops this idea. You might include

Pip's 'I want to be a gentleman on her account' (Chapter 17) to illustrate the romantic side of Pip's snobbery, or his recognition of Joe as 'this gentle Christian man' (Chapter 57) to show his final moral awareness. Other useful quotations might be Joe's view of Magwitch as a 'poor miserable fellow-creatur' (Chapter 5) or Pip's confession that the convict is 'a much better man than I had been to Joe' (Chapter 54). But three or four short quotations of this kind will be more than enough for an essay.

Quotation from the critics is not always necessary, but criticism may offer you a starting-point to develop or disagree with. In an essay on the theme of snobbery, you might quote Humphry House who says that in *Great Expectations* 'it is a remarkable achievement to have kept the reader's sympathy throughout a snob's progress'.* You could then go on to say that the story is *not* a 'snob's progress' but a progress away from snobbery. In an essay on characterisation you could use E.M. Forster's statement about 'flat' and 'round' characters and his conclusion that 'Dickens's people are nearly all flat'.† Your essay could then give examples of flat characters (Pumblechook, Mrs Joe, Wemmick) while using Pip to show that Dickens can also create a truly round and complex character. Remember that quoting a critic does not *prove* anything. You should use quotations from the critics only to sum up an interesting or possible opinion. It is your job to find the evidence for or against what the critic says.

Planning your answers

Do not start your essay until you have worked out a plan. There is no single plan that will fit all topics, but the following simple structure can be adapted to most answers.

(*a*) Introduction. A brief general statement about the topic, perhaps a famous critical opinion or a significant quotation from the novel. Problems raised by this statement.

(*b*) Discussion. Subdivisions dealing with different aspects of your topic, each one illustrated by concrete reference to the novel.

(*c*) Conclusion. Final comment on the topic in the light of your discussion. Refer back to your initial quotation and state how far you think it is valid.

Keep a careful balance between critical judgment and reference to the plot. Do not make broad generalisations without supporting them with evidence from the story. Do not simply retell the story without

*Humphry House. *The Dickens World*, Oxford University Press, London, 1961, p.155.
†E.M. Forster, *Aspects of the Novel*, Edward Arnold, London, 1927, pp.93–99.

drawing critical conclusions. Show that you are aware of possible objections to the views you put forward. Above all, be realistic about what you can hope to do in the time available. Keep your plan simple. Do not get lost in details. Allot space and time according to the relative importance of the topics you discuss. For example, in an essay on snobbery, Mrs Matthew Pocket is worth a sentence not a paragraph. In an essay on characterisation you might mention Wopsle, Pumblechook, and Mrs Joe as examples of caricature, but you would not have time to discuss all of them in detail.

Finally, remember that when you are asked to discuss a statement about the novel, you are not expected to express total agreement or disagreement. Look at the statement critically and try to think of the evidence both for and against it.

The essays given below do not represent the only correct answers to certain questions. They should serve you as examples of the structure we have just described.

Specimen questions and answers

The characters of Dickens are brilliant caricatures, but not complex and convincing individuals. Is this statement true with regard to *Great Expectations*?

The characters of Dickens are certainly vivid and memorable. Figures like Jaggers, Wemmick, Pumblechook, and Mrs Joe remain fixed in our minds by their gestures and speech-habits. But does this make them them convincing as real people? A famous modern novelist, E.M. Forster, has said that fictional characters are either 'round' or 'flat', and he concludes that most of Dickens's people are 'flat'.

Before we discuss this with regard to *Great Expectations*, we should note that flat characters are not necessarily insignificant. A novelist is not always concerned with psychological complexity: he may prefer to concentrate on social complexity. In presenting a complex picture of society, a variety of flat characters may be more effective than a few detailed psychological studies. This is often the case with Dickens.

The simple categories of flat and round, however, do less than justice to the variety of *Great Expectations*. The novel contains at least three types of character: (*a*) characters who are immediately revealed, (*b*) characters who are gradually revealed, (*c*) characters who develop.

The first type is obviously a caricature. Wopsle, Pumblechook, and Mrs Joe are immediately revealed by exaggerated physical features and gestures that tell us what to expect. Mrs Joe, for example, has a rough red skin, a stiff apron, and pins and needles stuck in her breast. We know from the start that she will be coarse, insensitive, and cruel. Wopsle's Roman nose, shining forehead, and deep voice establish him immediately as vain and theatrical. Pumblechook's behaviour at the Christmas dinner leaves us in no doubt about his character. We see his social pretensions in his pompous speech, his insensitivity in his comparison of Pip to a pig, his selfishness and vulgarity in the way he eats and drinks. Such characters immediately establish a pattern of behaviour that will not change throughout the novel. We feel that we know them already.

Our second group contains characters who are gradually revealed. Many of them seem, at first, to be caricatures. We notice Joe's confused syntax, Wemmick's post-office mouth, and Jaggers's habit of biting and throwing his forefinger. We think that we recognise Wemmick as an inhuman legal machine, Jaggers as a bullying lawyer, and Joe as a stupid good-natured man. But, in each case, we find that this view is too simple. Wemmick has a warm affectionate home life in his eccentric cottage where he releases all the humanity suppressed at the office. Jaggers has a guilty conscience (notice how he washes his hands) and has once tried to save a poor girl (Estella) from the misery of a criminal background. As for Joe, his apparent stupidity is shown as the result of his upbringing. His submission to Mrs Joe is not weakness but a sensitive reaction to the suffering of his mother. He has an inner confidence and a genuine pride in his profession as a blacksmith (see his speech to Pip during his first visit to London). Above all, we learn that Joe's good nature is not mere instinct but an intelligent and conscious moral response to experience. It cannot be said that Wemmick, Jaggers, and Joe develop during the novel. We do, however, learn a good deal more about them. They are not the caricatures they first seem to be.

Finally, there are characters who develop. Magwitch, when he first appears on the marshes, seems little more than a hungry suffering animal. On his return from Australia, he has already gained some dignity from his hard work and endurance, but he still has a negative view of humanity, seeing Pip largely as an instrument of revenge. By the end of the novel his dominant motive is love rather than revenge. He has developed to a point where he can reassure Pip and face death serenely. The most obviously developing character is, of course, Pip himself. To discuss Pip's development would require a long essay, but we can, at least, point to the subtle way Dickens shows his corruption by snobbery. Satis House forces him to recognise the fact of class distinction, making him ashamed of his coarse hands and thick boots. He surrenders to the romantic dream of becoming a gentleman for Estella's sake and becomes insensitive to the feelings of others (see his conversation with Biddy just before the news of his 'great expectations'). In the days of his good fortune he shows a callous neglect and misunderstanding of both Joe and Biddy, although he is constantly disturbed by feelings of guilt. He still has childish nightmares and romantic dreams which remind us of the continuity between the blacksmith's boy and the snobbish gentleman. Magwitch's return destroys Pip's illusions and thus releases the good instincts that have been frustrated but not destroyed by snobbery. Throughout the novel we see Pip's career as the complex result of external circumstances combined with inherent character. On the one hand, he is the victim of Miss Havisham's plots and of his chance meeting with Magwitch: on the other hand, his destiny is determined by his own characteristics of intelligence, imagination, introversion, and insecurity.

In conclusion, we must admit that not all the characters fit easily into our three categories. Estella is supposed to develop from heartlessness to love, but this development is not really shown in the novel. Nevertheless, *Great Expectations* as a whole shows that Dickens can approach character in many different ways, ranging from the comic caricature to the profound psychological portrait. The character of Pip alone is enough to prove that Dickens can create a complex character who is at least as memorable as his brilliant caricatures.

'It is a remarkable achievement to have kept the reader's sympathy throughout a snob's progress' (Humphry House). Discuss this comment on *Great Expectations*.

Snobbery is clearly the major theme of *Great Expectations* and, for much of the novel, Pip behaves like a snob. Humphry House's comment, however, raises two questions. First, how does Dickens keep our sympathy for Pip? Second, can the novel really be described as 'a snob's progress'?

Our initial sympathy for Pip is assured by the opening of the novel. He is an orphan, deprived of parental love and ill-treated by Mrs Joe who regards him as a burden. Joe, despite his good nature, is unable to protect him. Pip feels guilty and threatened, incapable of defending himself against the physical threats of Magwitch and the mental torture of Pumblechook's conversation. In character Pip is sensitive, imaginative and intelligent as we can see from his nightmares, from the story he invents after his visit to Satis House, and from his frustrated attempts at education. It is, perhaps, inevitable that such a boy should be dissatisfied with life at the forge.

Unfortunately, Pip's ambitions do not result in a gradual social progress through hard work. There are two reasons for this. First, he is brutally confronted with class distinction at Satis House where Estella, encouraged by Miss Havisham, despises his coarse hands and thick boots. He is too sensitive to ignore these insults and too insecure to fight against them. He is forced to accept the view that Satis House is superior to the forge. Second, his 'great expectations' come to him without warning and without explanation. The suddenness of his rise to gentility gives him no time to develop a mature moral standpoint. Moreover, we should remember that the society around him (Miss Havisham, Estella, Pumblechook, Trabb) encourages his snobbery. Against this majority the sound morality of Joe and Biddy stands little chance. To a large extent snobbery is forced on Pip by circumstances over which he has no control.

At the same time, it must be admitted that his behaviour is thoroughly unpleasant. He is tactless towards Biddy, forgetting how easy it is to hurt someone who is half in love with him. When he talks of raising Joe to a 'higher sphere', he cannot understand that Joe has his own pride as a blacksmith. Joe's visit to London is spoiled by Pip's awkwardness and embarrassment. He deliberately neglects to visit the forge and tries to compensate with condescending presents like the codfish and the barrel of oysters. Worst of all is his reaction to those who see through his snobbery: we remember his mean revenge on Trabb's boy and his anger with Biddy after Mrs Joe's funeral. Dickens, however, never allows Pip to seem hopelessly corrupt. Pip's main fault is that he thinks too much about himself, but this is natural in a boy who has been a lonely orphan. Moreover, Pip is often troubled by his conscience, as when he runs after Joe in London. We should not forget the romantic side of Pip's snobbery: he sees Estella as a princess and himself as a heroic knight. Such language shows that his snobbery is a youthful illusion rather than a deeply-rooted vice. Finally, it is clear that the mature narrator regrets his earlier snobbery. In all these ways Dickens keeps our sympathy with Pip even though we condemn his behaviour.

Magwitch's return releases Pip's better instincts by destroying the snobbish illusions that frustrated them. He now thinks first of other people, attempting to save Magwitch, urging Miss Havisham to help Herbert, and warning Estella against a disastrous marriage. It is essentially in serving the outcast Magwitch that Pip becomes worthy of Joe's forgiveness and able to recognise the blacksmith as a 'gentle Christian man'.

At this stage, it might be objected that the ending gives Pip everything a snob could desire: wealth, social status, and a beautiful wife. Here we must distinguish between snobbery and legitimate ambition. Dickens never suggests that Pip is wrong to seek a future outside the forge. His fault is to think that this future can come as a gift and that it justifies him in feeling superior. By his noble behaviour towards Magwitch he earns a second chance in life. Moreover, now that he is educated, it would be quite unrealistic to send him back to the forge. Eventually, he makes a modest fortune through his own hard work, but he no longer feels that money makes him superior. It is, therefore, misleading to speak of *Great Expectations* as 'a snob's progress': when Pip becomes a true gentleman, he ceases to be a snob. He exemplifies Matthew Pocket's statement that a true gentleman in manners must be a true gentleman at heart.

Part 5

Suggestions for further reading

The text

DICKENS, CHARLES: *Great Expectations*, edited by Angus Calder, Penguin Books, Harmondsworth, 1965. A fine critical introduction with useful notes.

Editions of other works by the author

Oliver Twist, edited by Kathleen Tillotson, Clarendon Press, Oxford, 1966.
David Copperfield, Oxford University Press, London, 1948.
Both novels concern the career of an orphan who overcomes a deprived childhood. *Oliver Twist* is a good example of Dickens's early manner. *David Copperfield* is largely autobiographical and offers grounds for comparison with *Great Expectations* as a first-person narrative.

General reading

CHESTERTON, G.K.: *Charles Dickens*, Methuen, London, 1906. The traditional view of Dickens as an exuberant comic genius.
FIELDING, K.J.: *Charles Dickens: A Critical Introduction*, Longmans, London, 1964. A comprehensive study by a major Dickens scholar.
FORSTER, E.M.: *Aspects of the Novel*, Edward Arnold, London, 1927. Contains the distinction between flat and round characters.
HOBSBAUM, PHILIP: *A Reader's Guide to Charles Dickens*, Thames and Hudson, London, 1972. Dickens as a social critic speaking for the individual against the system.
HOUSE, HUMPHRY: *The Dickens World*, Oxford University Press, London, 1961. The best discussion of Dickens in relation to the Victorian background.
JOHNSON, EDGAR: *Charles Dickens: His Tragedy and Triumph*, Gollancz, London, 1953. The definitive modern biography.
HILLIS MILLER, J.: *Charles Dickens: The World of his Novels*, Harvard University Press, Cambridge, Massachusetts, 1958. Contains a discussion of Pip as the archetypal Dickens hero in search of identity.

ORWELL, GEORGE: 'Charles Dickens' in *Inside the Whale*, Secker and Warburn, London, 1940; reprinted in *Decline of the English Murder and Other Essays*, Penguin, Harmondsworth, 1965. An influential short appreciation by a major modern writer.

VAN GHENT, DOROTHY: *The English Novel: Form and Function*, Holt, Rinehart and Winston, New York, 1953. Contains a good chapter on Dickens's use of symbolism in *Great Expectations*.

WALL, STEPHEN: editor, *Charles Dickens: A Critical Anthology*, Penguin Books, Harmondsworth, 1970. A comprehensive collection of criticism from Victorian times to the present day, including extracts from most of the material listed above.

The author of these notes

ANTHONY MORTIMER graduated in English from the University of Leeds, and obtained his doctorate from Case Western Reserve University (U.S.A.). He has taught at universities in Yugoslavia, Italy, Germany, and the United States. He now lives in Switzerland where he lectures at the University of Geneva and is Professor at the University of Fribourg. His previous publications include *Modern English Poets: Five Introductory Essays* (1966), *Petrarch's Canzoniere in the English Renaissance* (1975), and *Petrarch: Selected Poems* (1977).